Empowering the Soul
Creating Harmony
in a Troubled World

Empowering the Soul
Creating Harmony
in a Troubled World

A Collection of Essays Exploring
Global Healing and Spiritual Well-Being

Introduction by Pandit Rajmani Tigunait, Ph.D.

HIMALAYAN INSTITUTE®
PRESS
Honesdale, Pennsylvania

Himalayan Institute Press
952 Bethany Turnpike
Honesdale, PA 18431
www.HimalayanInstitute.org

First Printing, 2007

Printed in the USA.

The paper used in this publication meets the minimum requirements of American National Standard of Information Sciences—Permanence of Paper for Printed Library Materials, ANSI Z39.48-1984.

Library of Congress Cataloging-in-Publication Data

Empowering the soul: a collection of essays exploring global healing and spiritual well-being / introduction by Pandit Rajmani Tigunait. p. cm.

Summary: "Compilation of essays presenting advice on a wide range of topics including holistic methods for healthy living, the role of media in public perception, peace through diplomacy, and other issues for personal and global enrichment"—Provided by publisher.

Includes bibliographical references and index.

    ISBN-13: 978-0-89389-261-6 (alk. paper)
    ISBN-10: 0-89389-261-0 (alk. paper)

1. Yoga. 2. Meditation. 3. Spiritual life. 4. Nonviolence. 5. Peace.   I. Tigunait, Rajmani, 1953-   .

B132.Y6E527 2006
181'.45—dc22

2006020270

Contents

Foreword

NELSON ROCKEFELLER, GRANDSON OF THE richest man in America, was once asked, "Nelson, how much is enough money?" And he had the perfect answer: "Just a little bit more." My own experience over the last fifteen years illustrates this thinking; it is really the essence of what we all suffer from to some extent in this country and in the so-called Western world. We believe that being successful means making a lot of money. I followed that code heartily for fifteen years, and I was successful. I founded a company that has grown from two people fourteen years ago to more than twenty-five hundred people today, and it's still growing. I'd made a lot of money and was supposedly successful. The problem was that I was miserable. I was absolutely miserable. I was at the pinnacle of my life in many ways—successful in business beyond my wildest dreams, going public with a major company that I had founded, and still a young man. Yet inside I felt empty and unsatisfied.

I tried to figure out what was missing and realized I was all business, all money, all for myself only. That's the way I had lived for fifteen years. You achieve your goals. You feel hollow, so you raise the bar. You achieve those goals and you still feel hollow, so you raise the bar again. I completely ignored a spiritual life to go along with my moneymaking life. Ironically, at the pinnacle of my supposed success, I was the most unhappy and empty I have ever been.

And I know there are many like me in the world. Today my personal computer has more memory and power than a multimillion-dollar IBM mainframe that would have filled my entire office twenty-five years ago. As a society, we are accomplished beyond our wildest dreams in the realm of technology. Yet we have paid a great price. We are living in the wealthiest country in the world, but our materialism seems to pull us further from our own truths.

Luckily, I met some wonderful people about that time and went about changing my life. My biggest good fortune came not from my business accomplishments, but rather from my discovery of the Himalayan Institute and its Sacred Link mission at that crucial time in my life. I started thinking about the real meaning and purpose in life, about spiritual principles. I started to meditate, exercise every day, and watch my diet. I began to try to be humble, to consider the needs of others, and to think of my life as service and not ego indulgence. I recognized that I had been living life for my personal advancement only and that I had the means and resources to do much more for the world, to do something good for the world. I realized that my own peace and happiness rested on my previously ignored inner life—the voice of kindness, compassion, and selfless service—and that by giving to the world in accordance with my skills and talents, I could chip away at my own inner unhappiness.

I still forget sometimes, but I really do believe our careers and work and our families and friends are here to provide opportunities for us to transform ourselves, to let go of our selfishness. Success to me now is happiness, the kind of happiness that, no matter what the circumstances, cannot be taken away, the kind of happiness that comes from sharing the best of yourself and your work.

This is the message of Sacred Link, and in one way or another, this is the theme of the stories you will read in this book from courageous people working in all areas of life. These are people who are working, each in his or her own way, to create a peaceful, sustainable world of prosperity. What is so great about the ideas in this book, and the conference that spawned it, is that it is contagious. It's kind of like the one-hundredth-monkey effect. If we can all create enough good intentions and actions in our businesses and in our lives, sooner or later that starts to become the norm. What a wonderful thing to work for.

Marc Vaccaro
Cofounder
Great Lakes Companies
Great Wolf Resorts

Introduction
Creating Harmony in a Troubled World

Pandit Rajmani Tigunait, Ph.D.

Spiritual head of the Himalayan Institute, Pandit Rajmani Tigunait, Ph.D., is the successor of Sri Swami Rama. He holds two doctorates, one from the University of Allahabad in India and the other from the University of Pennsylvania. He is a regular contributor to *Yoga + Joyful Living* magazine; the author of numerous books, including the best-selling *At the Eleventh Hour;* and is the force behind Sacred Link™—The Healing Revolution.

THE HIMALAYAN INSTITUTE HAS FOR decades sought to create a bridge between ancient wisdom and modern technology, between spirituality and science, and between East and West. The Institute's Sacred Link program was launched in 2001 in an effort to put into action the tenets of yoga philosophy and to create a vision for global healing and spiritual well-being. In addition to educational, environmental, and humanitarian programs, the Sacred Link program organizes conferences that bring together pioneers in this healing revolution, be they alternative energy experts, diplomats, business executives, attorneys, yoga teachers, or holistic health practitioners. This book grew out of the first Sacred Link conference, held at the Himalayan Institute headquarters in Honesdale, Pennsylvania, in 2004. The success of that conference, the keen insights of the speakers, and the overall vision of hope that emerged at the end of this gathering sparked the idea for a book that could reach an even wider audience and stand as a lasting vision of a more peaceful and compassionate world. I hope that this collection of essays will inspire you as they have inspired me. To the stories and experiences recounted in these pages I would like to add a few reflections of my own, which may explain the genesis of the Sacred Link.

I was born in a tiny village tucked away in the interior of rural India, a region drowning in illiteracy, poverty, inequality, social injustice, and oppression. Village life was a life of hardship. Using primitive tools, villagers plowed their land, raised their cattle, wove their clothes, built their huts, and trained themselves in their family trades. Calamities were a normal part of life. Famine, flood, drought, and epidemics of cholera, malaria, and smallpox visited them frequently. Yet they were people of high spirit, resilient and optimistic. They accepted their losses as part of life. Infused with faith in Providence, they were convinced that their hard work and God's grace would fill their future with bounty. To them, everything that happened in life had a higher purpose and meaning. Thus, they bounced back after each calamity and, with renewed vigor, invested themselves fully in the celebration of life. Observing this as a young man, I concluded that joy is an innate and priceless virtue of the spirit.

When I came to the United States in the 1980s, the glamour and grandeur of this mighty nation overwhelmed me. The moment I arrived at Kennedy airport, sensory overload from the dazzling lights made me freeze in shock. I was stunned by four-lane highways, New York's skyscrapers, the Lincoln Tunnel, and by human beings three times the size of my Indian body. I marveled at everything I saw and thanked God for bringing me to this land of limitless possibility.

I had not yet recovered from the shock of the new

world when I was appointed spiritual director of the Himalayan Institute. Assuming this role, I made a discovery that shocked me even more. Most of the people who came to seek my advice on spiritual matters were seeking meaning and purpose in life and had a common complaint: "I am not happy with myself. I'm confused. I don't know what to do with my life." Their complaints made no sense to me. They came from affluent families and had everything they needed to live a comfortable life. They had cars, houses, jobs, and financial security. They were part of a wonderful country with very little religious conflict, ethnic violence, political instability, or financial instability. Yet they were full of anxiety and fear. What were they afraid of? Why were they so full of doubt? What had shaken their conviction in themselves? In this land of freedom and opportunity, who were they trying to protect themselves from? What were they afraid of losing?

Since then, twenty-five years of traveling and teaching have confirmed my impression of a world run by fear. I see people overwhelmed by a pervasive sense of uncertainty, insecurity, and doubt. Who are these people? In most cases, they are intelligent and materially successful. In all worldly matters they are achievers. In their fields of expertise, they are competent and confident, yet they are struggling with private demons—anger, hatred, desire, aversion, egotism, and a sense of unworthiness—all leading to confusion and inner restlessness.

Meanwhile, the world I left behind twenty-five years ago began to catch up with the Western model of living—work hard, accumulate possessions, and let your faith in a higher reality gradually fade away. Calamities like famine, cholera, malaria, and plague visit less frequently, thanks to the advancement of modern medicine. Markets are flooded with necessities as well as with amenities and the population as a whole has better access to education. And yet, discontent stalks the land. Both rich and poor have become hungrier—the rich are hungry for all the things the West has and the poor remain hungry for the basic necessities of life. What happened to the people of my motherland? I wondered. Who took away their faith and their inner joy, the priceless gift of the spirit?

At the beginning of the twenty-first century, I hear more loudly than ever the voice of my master, Swami Rama, and many others who came before him: "To be born a human being is the greatest gift, and to die without experiencing the fullness of life is the greatest loss." How many of us have experienced or are even trying to experience the fullness of life? Some are busy grabbing power and position while others run after the short-lived charms of the world; and neither really knows where this race will end. One thing is sure, however: they are exhausted yet still pushing harder to reach what always seems to be just out of reach. Still others belittle this world, trivialize material success, and, to escape the empty nature of worldly achievement, resort exclusively to the inner journey that they call spirituality. Both groups suffer from fragmentation, exclusivity, isolation, and their "either this or that" attitude. What they have in common is the perpetual hunger for experiencing the fullness of life.

I also recall vividly Swamiji's proclamation, "Only after knowing ourselves at every level can we aspire to reclaim life in its fullness. Only after experiencing life in its fullness can lasting joy be ours." For centuries, the East invested in spiritual pursuits, ignoring the reality of the physical world, and as a result suffered from material poverty. The West has been intent on accumulating material riches while ignoring the vast territory of the spirit. Now it is clear that both hemispheres have shut themselves off to half of reality. The result is that today, one is trying to run after what the other is trying to run from.

The process of integration and living with greater ease, peace, and dignity must first begin at the personal level. No transformation can ever take off without self-transformation. No unhappy person can ever make others happy. No empty person can grant fulfillment to others. Only after we have collected the missing pieces of our private world and arranged them in harmonious unity will our emptiness vanish and fulfillment follow. The resulting contentment will bring lasting joy. This is what the ancient masters called yoga, the path of union and integration.

> To live a joyful life is the greatest accomplishment. Failure to live joyfully is the greatest loss.

The kind of yoga I am talking about is more than asana and breathing exercises. It is more than all those styles of asana in the market. I am talking about the path of integration and unity of which today's popular yoga is just a small part. Asana is good; it will bring flexibility to your limbs. Pranayama, the breathing exercises, are good; they will strengthen your nervous system. Ayurveda is good; it will help balance your *doshas*. Pancha karma is good; it will detoxify your organs. Organic food is good; it will nurture your body. Aromatherapy is good; it will soothe your senses. Chanting is good; it will relieve your emotional build-up. Rituals are good; they will fill space with sacredness. Similarly, the practice of surrender will soften your ego. Selfless service will enable you to build a healthy family and society, and your selfless love will pave the way to experiencing divine presence here and now. But these are only à la carte practices on the menu. Experiencing the fullness of life requires that we offer ourselves something more than piecemeal services.

Again I quote Swami Rama, "A human being is not body nor mind alone. A human being is a combination of both, and much more. Every individual is a nucleus of his family, society, nation, and all of humanity. Every individual is an integral part of the intricate web of life. What good is yoga, meditation, spirituality, and holistic health if it doesn't introduce you to yourself—your body, breath, and mind? What good is the practice that doesn't help you become a healthier and happier person? What good is knowledge that doesn't make you a more loving and kind person? What good is your life if you remain useless to yourself and useless to the rest of the world? You can master asana and turn your body into a pretzel and still carry a confused mind on your shoulders. I call that useless yoga. You can practice meditation for hours and still remain a victim of your fear, doubt, anger, and sadness. I call that useless meditation. You can practice spirituality by visiting temples and churches and still suffer from inner emptiness. I call that useless spirituality. You are a useful, wonderful, and beautiful person. You can infuse others with the same wonder and beauty, provided you have first reclaimed them yourself. This is what great masters have taught, and this is what I wish people of the modern world could learn."

I studied with this great master, Swami Rama, for years. I gave 100 percent of myself to the practice he taught me. I did everything that I could do to grow spiritually; I spent hours meditating daily. I committed myself to a good, healthy diet. I practiced hatha yoga and pranayama. Hoping to tap into the fresh and peaceful energy of the early hours, I woke up at three in the morning, a routine that lasted for a decade. And yet, I was not satisfied with my progress. I wished to have a more clear, calm, tranquil, and one-pointed mind. I wished to be more compassionate and kind-hearted. I was still the victim of my occasional temper. In desperation one day I put my problem before Swamiji. The answer he gave cleared my mind and opened my heart. Some of my problems may still exist, but my complaints about them are long gone, freeing me to attend to both my worldly matters and spiritual pursuits.

Swamiji said to me, "The source of your problem lies in the vast field of collective consciousness. Millions of people pass their nights with hunger. Billions struggle day and night just to remain barely alive. They lack the bare necessities of life—food, clothes, shelter. Anger and grief oozing from their pores has seeped into the entire web of life and penetrated the building blocks of all life—food, water, and air. We are eating food, drinking water, and breathing air that contains subtle energy of the painful sighs of the destitute. Rich and poor, Easterners and Westerners, men and women, and meditators and nonmeditators alike, including you and me, are consuming the same food, water, and air. The final degree of inner unrest that you are experiencing will stay with you until this world becomes a more loving and kind place."

At first, what he said sounded grim and hopeless. But as I reflected on his words, a realization dawned at the level beyond my intellect. Just as we cannot live in isolation from the rest of the world, personal peace and happiness cannot exist in isolation from the peace and happiness of others. Everyone on this planet shares one breath and one life force. The air that we exhale contains the subtle properties of every single cell of our body, as well as our thoughts, feelings, likes and dislikes, desires, and frustrations. The very same air is inhaled by others around the globe. Thus, we are constantly sharing each other's input and output.

The latter half of the twentieth century brought an unprecedented level of growth and development. Industrial output today is beyond the imagination of an average person. But only a few million upper-class and a billion or so middle-class consumers make up the global market. The remaining billions struggle just to collect the crumbs. One and a half billion people in China and India alone are living below the poverty level. Hundreds of millions of migrant workers in these two countries float between villages and towns in a futile attempt to find jobs. More than five million children every year die of malnutrition. Forty million HIV/AIDS patients are simply left at the mercy of a slow death. The condition of women in Asia and Africa is flatly disgraceful to humanity.

It's as if billions of hearts like mini factories are pouring clouds of pain, agony, fear, insecurity, anger, and violence into the planet's atmosphere. These clouds travel all around the globe, influencing the minds and hearts of everyone, including those who seem far removed from the destitute. The United States of America, for example, today enjoys the great prosperity. Its military can obliterate its enemies in a matter of hours, and yet it is one of the most fear-run societies. Security issues dictate both national and international policies.

Today, people in every corner of the world, from East to West, in developed countries and developing countries, in Himalayan caves and the high-rise buildings of New York and Tokyo, all have equally agitated minds. This doesn't make sense unless we see and feel the interconnected nature of every soul on the planet. The art of joyful living can become a reality only when we work together to eliminate each other's hunger, be it hunger for food, or hunger for power. The gap between the poor and rich, East and West, and men and women, has to be reduced. We must find ways to make the external world conducive to our inner journey, and the social atmosphere conducive to personal transformation; and we must balance personal fulfillment with the higher welfare of the larger world. This is the essence of yoga, the path of union and integration, and the ground for joyful living. I hope the essays of this book will bring you the ideas, as well as the tools and means, for personal transformation, social regeneration, and enlightened leadership.

Myths That Pass for Truths

Deborah Willoughby

As founding editor of *Yoga International* magazine and the editor of *Yoga + Joyful Living*, Deborah Willoughby has consistently provided an alternative to the mainstream media's vision of the world for nearly two decades. After completing an M.A. in literature, she honed her editorial savvy in Washington, D.C., working for the Department of Justice, the Environmental Protection Agency, the United States Information Agency, and the Council on Environmental Quality, among others. President and longtime resident of the Himalayan Institute, she regularly teaches in meditation seminars.

ONCE UPON A TIME, AS THE STORYTELLERS say, we as a species got all of our information directly. We got it from the clergy and from our friends, and most of all we got it from our direct experience of living in the world. And the world we were living in was a natural world. Until very recently, most of the people on this planet lived in rural areas. Most of us earned our living by agriculture, and most of the rest were still living in villages and on farms and thus had a deep connection to nature. That was our primary source of information. And how we get information matters. Humans are meaning-making creatures. We live in our interpretation of the world, and this interpretation shapes our present and creates our future.

During the last century, the same time that humanity was making the transition from being primarily rural to being primarily urban, another transformation occurred: our sources of information shifted from personal, direct experience to newspapers, magazines, and the electronic media. Now most of our information about the world comes from the media in general and from television in particular. You are probably familiar with the statistics: Ninety-nine percent of American homes have television. More American homes have television than have plumbing. That's still true. In Appalachia they may not have indoor plumbing, but they have a television. The television is on for seven hours a day in the average American home. That doesn't mean we watch it all the time; some of the time it's just wallpaper background—constant, constant, constant information being beamed at us. The average American watches television four hours a day. Of course, some of us watch considerably less, but what I'm talking about is the whole culture—an average of four hours a day. Television creates our shared reference. For all practical purposes, if something isn't reported or presented on television, it doesn't exist in our social consciousness. Television has become our witness. It's our shared vehicle for knowing what we know and for understanding who we are. I'm going to submit that this is a problem. We are creating a future that we may not want to be walking into.

I read that an IBM executive in the course of a conversation with Marshall McLuhan said, "My children lived more of life by the time they were in first grade than my grandparents did." He meant that because of the information his kids were getting from television, they had lived more. He was equating the information with living. It's undoubtedly true that his kids had more information about the world than his grandparents had. I'm sure that the average eighth-grader who watches prime-time television knows more about certain aspects of human sexual behavior than my grandmother ever dreamed of. But does that eighth-grader know that potatoes grow underground?

Does that child know how to find the North Star? What it means when there's a ring around the moon? Can that child distinguish a meadowlark from a white-breasted nuthatch? Probably not. He may have more information than my grandmother had, but it is information of a different kind. And there's a huge loss of information that we're not acknowledging.

All spiritual teachers in all traditions tell us over and over that what we do and what we see every day shapes us. A significant percentage of what we see every day—the information that we get every day—comes from television. And television presents a coherent vision of the world. The question is, is it a vision that is likely to create the kind of future that we're hoping for? I suspect that most of us want essentially the same things. We want a peaceful world. We want to live without fear. We want to be able to pass on to our kids a planet that's healthy, and we want them to have a pleasant, healthy, sustainable future. So the question is, does television support us in creating that kind of world?

There's a lot of reading and a lot of writing and a lot of research about television. Researchers often talk about television as both a mirror and a window. It's the way we see the world and the way we see ourselves. By looking at our televisions, we're seeing the larger world and we also are seeing ourselves to some extent. We understand that. But I don't think we understand the shaping power this has. Television

The average American multitasks 70 percent of the time. Speed becomes a habit. When we're rushing around trying to balance a host of competing demands, we see only the fragmented, turbulent surface of life, not the vast interconnected web of relationships that supports that surface.

shapes our reality. Let's take a quick look at three different ways it does that: violence, speed, and craving.

Violence

You may be familiar with the catchphrase "If it bleeds, it leads." Watch your local news at night and you'll see that almost all of the stories have to do with fires, car crashes, some form of violent assault, or robbery. Forty to 50 percent of the news reported on television has that kind of content. Only 3 percent of all crime involves violence, but 45 to 50 percent of the evening news coverage focuses on violence. Why? Two reasons. It is cheap and it is easy to report.

It's a lot easier to take a camera to a fire than it is to cover a public hearing on land use, for instance. And, of course, coverage of lurid events attracts viewers. And that's the name of the game—getting as many viewers as you can. As a result of this kind of reporting, people get the idea that the world is much more violent than it really is. Then add in the post-CNN reality. You've got on-spot cameras all the time. If something happens—for instance, a child kidnapping—you've got a camera right there in the face of the sobbing parents and distraught neighbors. Because of the heartbreaking nature of the crime, all the major networks pick up the story. For the next several days—until something more disturbing comes along—it will be the leading news story every day. That gives viewers the sense that these kinds of tragedies are happening all the time. The fact is that kidnapping of children by strangers is a very rare crime and the number of cases has been decreasing during the past twenty years. But that is not our impression.

The other thing is that, as the population ages, as people retire and have more leisure time, they spend more time watching CNN, MSNBC, and FOX News—the around-the-clock news programs. In a world of six billion people, there's always something on fire or surrounded by officers in SWAT uniforms. The camera loves drama. You can be instantly anyplace in the world. So you're seeing these tragedies all the time. All the time. It gives the impression that violence has spiraled out of control.

To what extent do we separate reality from the world presented on television? Of course we do to an extent, but there's an extent to which we don't. I'll give you a personal example. My mom is eighty-six years old. She lives in a small town in western Colorado with a population of around thirty thousand. She hates television so she doesn't watch it. She goes to church, to the senior center, to doctors' appointments and leaves the house unlocked—and doesn't think a thing of it. She goes to sleep at night with both the front and back doors unlocked. In the summertime she sometimes won't even close the outside door. Why? Because she doesn't feel threatened. She's lived in that town for twenty-five years and she's never known anybody who's been robbed, raped, or mugged, and she feels perfectly safe. She is not a naïve woman. She lived in the suburbs of Washington, D.C. She lived in the suburbs of Denver. She lived in the suburbs of Minneapolis. It's not like she's some country bumpkin and doesn't know what the world is. But her direct experience of her world is that she's perfectly safe.

Her next-door neighbor has the television on all the time. I've never been in Marion's house when the television isn't on. Marion is beside herself because Mom won't lock her door so she calls me: "Deborah, I'm not sure your mother should be living alone. She went to sleep last night and left her doors unlocked." Now I ask you, who has the more realistic view of the world—Mom or her neighbor?

The point is, the more violence we see on television, the more we feel threatened by violence. Studies have shown a direct correlation between the quantity of television watched and our general fearfulness about the world. Heavy viewers believe the world to be much more dangerous than light viewers do. And, this overestimation of crime is amplified by the fact that 45 percent of the crimes reported in the media involve sex or violence, although only 3 percent of crimes actually involve sex or violence.

Now, if you factor in the entertainment portion to the nightly news, the feeling that the world is a scary place absolutely shoots up. On April 7, 1994, the Center for Media and Public Affairs monitored everything shown on television in Washington, D.C., on that day. There were 2,604 acts of violence pictured on that one day alone. This amplifies our feeling that the world is really violent. It creates fear. This is particularly true for women. In entertainment television, for every white male who is a victim of violence there are thirty-nine women who are victims of violence. The result is that women have a grossly exaggerated view of how likely they are to become victims of a violent crime. There was a study at the University of Sheffield in England a couple of years ago showing that most American women believe that they are likely to be the victim of a violent crime sometime in their lifetime when in fact the odds are very, very low. So we walk around feeling threatened. We have an amplified sense of fear that the facts don't bear out.

> Spiritual teachers in all traditions tell us over and over that what we do and what we see every day shapes us. A significant percentage of what we see every day—the information that we get every day—comes from television.

From the 1960s to the 1990s violence rose rapidly, but it leveled off in 1990 and has been falling ever since. I'll give you some quick statistics: Homicides fell by 75 percent in San Diego, 70 percent in New York City, and by big margins in Boston, Baltimore, Los Angeles, and other cities. In fact, in 2002 the total number of homicides in New York City was equal to the total number of homicides there in 1963 in spite of the fact that the population of New York City has skyrocketed. But we watch *NYPD Blue, Law & Order,* and all these police programs and we think the streets of New York are really dangerous. In 2002 New York City had a lower crime rate than most rural states. But that's not what we think. This massive wash of violence coming at us through our screens not only undermines our sense of well-being, it also creates aggressive behavior. There are countless longitudinal studies, studies that follow one population over time, and they show that the more violence children watch on television, the more likely they are to be aggressive when they grow up.

One researcher studied eight-year-old boys in a small town in New York, beginning in 1960. He logged how much television and which kind of television they watched. When he came back in 1971, the boys were nineteen, and he discovered that the more violent television they had watched, the more likely they were to have been in trouble with the law. He came back again when they were thirty and found that those who had watched the most television violence when they were eight inflicted more violent punishments on their children, were convicted of more serious crimes, and were reported to be more aggressive than those who had watched less television or less violent television. TV shapes our character. It makes us become more aggressive.

In addition to undermining our sense of safety and creating aggressive behavior, all of this violence that we see in our homes creates the impression that aggressive behavior is normal. The University of Pennsylvania's George Gerbner says that all of this violence militarizes the mind and leads to what he calls the mean-world syndrome. It's a mean, nasty world. Better watch out. Because television projects the world as worse than it is, at least for the middle and upper classes, we become anxious and therefore more willing to depend on authority, strong police measures, gated communities, all that kind of authoritarian protopolicing going on today. This has a serious consequence for those of us who are interested in helping create a more peaceful, fulfilling world.

Finally, television influences the decisions we make at the polls. Gerbner says, "Living in a sea of violent images breeds aggressiveness in some but it breeds desensitization, insecurity, mistrust, and anger in most people. Punitive and vindictive actions against dark forces in a mean world are made to look appealing, especially when it's presented as quick and decisive and enhancing our self-control." How was it that we got into Iraq? Strike first. Take care of yourself. Get rid of the bad guy. But television doesn't ponder the consequences of this violence. In the *Devi Mahatmyam* there is a demon called Raktabija. When you attack this demon (think Saddam Hussein), every drop of blood from every cut you inflict on him falls to the ground and becomes another warrior. Violence breeds violence— humans have understood this for millennia, but nobody is telling us that anymore.

Another way that television influences our decisions at the polls and the actions of our elected officials is that heavy viewers of television (and I would say four hours a day is pretty heavy) favor more law-and-order measures. They tend to favor capital punishment and three-strike prison sentences. They're always for building new prisons and imprisoning more people. Look what happened with the assault weapons ban. Who in their right mind thinks we need assault weapons on the street? I listened to some interviews on a prime-time news show with people on the street about why they oppose banning assault weapons. They don't feel safe and think they need AK-47s and Uzis to protect themselves. We can shake our heads at this, but it is a deeply held belief. The information they have about the world tells them that this is true. Therefore Congress wasn't even willing to discuss the assault weapons ban. So what happens when people see a lot of violence on television is that the world does indeed become a more dangerous place. You have people running around on the streets with Uzis. Does that make you feel safe?

Speed

As Marshall McLuhan told us, "The medium is the message." The medium of television is speed. Television is fast. Rapid-fire imagery, speedy dialogue, quick camera edits. The average shot in an entertainment program is 3.5 seconds. The average shot in a commercial is 2.5 seconds. We've got this stuff coming at us—blink, blink, blink, blink, blink. And we've been having it coming at us at this speed for so long—it's actually speeding up—that we're used to it. We think that's normal.

In television, time is literally money. Let's have a little digression here and talk about what television really is for. Its purpose is not to give us the news. It's not to entertain us. Its purpose is to sell products. Television is controlled by advertising revenue. Its principal function is to deliver audiences to advertisers. The more popular a program is, obviously, the more money it can charge its advertisers for commercials.

Not all countries have commercial television. In 1987 most of the countries in the European Union had perhaps one commercial television station and the rest of their programming was government controlled. That's got some other issues, but when Austria was thinking about making the switch to commercial TV, they invited Neil Postman, a social critic and a media expert, to come to Austria to tell them what they could expect if they shifted from government-controlled television, which has a few commercials and focuses on matters of public interest, to commercial television. This is what he said to them:

> To make programs popular you need fast-paced, visually dynamic programs with an emphasis on interesting images rather than on serious content. This means an increase in comedy, car chases, violence, and sexually oriented material. As audiences come to expect fast-paced, visually exciting programs, they will begin to find issue-oriented public affairs news programs dull. To compete with entertainment programs, news and public affairs programs will become more visual and more personality oriented. As a result, there will be a decline in the public's capacity to understand and discuss events in a serious way.

Again, the shaping power. In the coverage of the 1968 political conventions, a sound bite was 42.5 seconds long. That's still pretty short for a complex idea but it's close to a minute. In 1988 it was 9.5 seconds. Now how are you going to say anything meaningful in 9 seconds?

The other thing that's happened is that commercials have gotten shorter and faster. Before 1971 commercials were 60 seconds long. In 1971 Madison Avenue realized that faster-paced television ads could make the same pitch in half the time, so they shortened the television commercials to 30 seconds almost overnight. By the 1980s a lot of commercials were 15 seconds. So we have a constant acceleration, into I don't know what—warp speed? Escape velocity? Speed is the enemy of reflection. You can't think clearly when you are moving fast.

The average American multitasks 70 percent of the time. Speed becomes a habit. I'm not saying television created this, but we're living in this fast-paced environment—crazy, careering out of control, and television certainly contributes to this feeling. When we're racing around and multitasking, we see only what's right in front of us. Our vision is restricted to what contributes to solving our immediate problem—how to make more money, how to produce more energy, how to save a little time. The long-term effects are ignored. We'll deal with them later when we have more time, we tell ourselves. But we never have time. When we're rushing around trying to balance a host of competing demands, we see only the fragmented, turbulent surface of life, not the vast interconnected web of relationships that supports that surface.

The fast pace of living affects not only adults but children as well, and television only compounds the damage. In 1950 the average fourteen-year-old had a vocabulary of twenty-five thousand words. In 1999 that figure had dropped to ten thousand. If you don't have a rich and varied vocabulary, there are many things that you can't express. There are ideas you can't have. There are plans you can't make.

Younger children are also susceptible. The prestigious *Journal of Pediatrics* recently did a study showing that exposure to television can damage the brain of a one- to three-year-old. There's a strong direct correlation between the number of hours that a child that age watches television and attention deficit hyperactivity disorder (ADHD) when he or she is seven. The number of American children taking Ritalin and similar drugs to treat ADHD or to improve school performance tripled between 1985 and 1996. It's now at least 6 percent of American children. Even taking into account inappropriate diagnoses, there's no question that exposure to fast-paced television is damaging to children.

Craving

In 2002 annual advertising expenditure was $247 billion in the United States alone. Not all of that is for television, but a lot of it is. Advertising is arguably the most persuasive and multifarious form of communication from which the modern public gets its beliefs about what makes life healthy, satisfying, and sustainable in the long run. More people now get their information about what prescription drugs to take from advertising than they do from their doctors. We're barraged with messages both subliminal and overt on billboards, magazines, television, and in the movies telling us that everything we're looking for in life can be found in a car, a bowl of ice cream, a perfect vacation. The hidden message is that what we own or what we wear has the power to endow us with self-respect.

When Neil Postman was talking to the Austrians, he emphasized that commercials stress the values of youth, consumption, immediate gratification, the love for what is new, and the contempt for what is old. "Television screens saturated with commercials promote the utopian and childish ideal that all problems have fast, simple, and technological solutions," he told them. It's not only the advertisements. Look at the sitcoms. Most television characters don't possess many skills. They can tend bar; they can solve crimes. That's pretty much it. Virtually no one in comedy or drama is shown actually working, but they have great apartments, terrific clothes, they're young, happy, attractive. Just by virtue of its omnipresence, television constantly reinforces certain ideas. The purpose of our lives is to have more things, to experience more sensations, to have fun, to become richer, more powerful, more famous.

> Most of what comes out of our television sets is based on an untested hypothesis: By the constant and universal application of technology, we can improve the quality of our lives.
>
> By producing and consuming more and more things, we can find inner fulfillment. This leads to a frenzy of economic activity not based on human needs or the needs of the environment but on an unexamined addiction to profit.

And we have to protect ourselves from a host of troubles. It's not only the violence in the news and the violence in the programming that makes us think we have to protect ourselves. That message is also imbedded in television commercials. The other night I made a point of watching six commercials. Five of the six commercials were telling me I should be afraid of something. As a woman over fifty, I need to be afraid of heart attacks. We all need to be afraid of nail fungus and of sun damage to our eyes. And, of course, in order to protect myself I need to buy some products—transition lenses, for example. This is a constant message. In addition to making us more anxious, these commercials lead us to confuse wants with needs. What do we really need? A warm, comfortable place to sleep. Nourishing food. Clean water. A few clothes that are clean and comfortable. That's really all we need. But wants are endless, and television just creates an endless train of wants.

There was a time when middle-class people and poor people didn't see how the rich lived. Now we see it all the time. It would never have occurred to a farmer fifty years ago to want a yacht, but now we see all that stuff. It looks great. We want it. The average American household has eight thousand dollars' worth of credit-card debt. Television lures us into debt, but more than that, it gives us a false idea of where happiness lies.

Television feeds myths about money, youth, and the value of vengeance. The more money you have, the happier you are, television would lead us to believe. It's true that money correlates to happiness to a certain degree. As you rise out of poverty and approach the middle class, happiness increases. No question. But once you reach the middle class, happiness decouples from money. Millionaires are no happier than middle-class people. Beyond a certain point, money and happiness have no correlation at all.

The next myth deals with youth—the idea is that young is better, happier, more fun. Do anything to stay young or to look young. The truth is that people over fifty have a greater sense of contentment and well-being than the young. Youth and happiness do not correlate. Age and happiness correlate, but television is never going to tell you that.

The third myth is based on the idea of vengeance. Trends in everything—education, law, politics, media systems—all urge us to view ourselves as wronged by various forces, real or imagined, to get angry and fight back, to fixate on harms done to us and to search for the perpetrators. We're encouraged to even the score with those who may or may not have wronged us, using litigation, bad publicity, any means. Don't get mad, get even. Get even—you'll feel better. That's a lie. It's not even remotely true. Research shows that those who forgive others are happier, healthier people who live longer, more successful lives. Conversely, those who don't forgive have more stress-related disorders, lower immune function, and higher rates of cardiovascular disease and depression than the population as a whole.

So the problem with the electronic media is that it promotes violence, speeds us up, increases cravings, and encourages us to confuse wants with needs. But an even more fundamental problem is that it alters perception. Perception is a form of physiological intake, just like food and water. That's what yoga would tell you. You are what you see. And television alters the perception of what it means to be human. And this is not going to create the kind of world that we're hoping for. Most of what comes out of our television sets is based on an untested hypothesis: By the constant and universal application of technology, we can improve the quality of our lives. By producing and consuming more and more things, we can find inner fulfillment. This leads to a frenzy of economic activity not based on human needs or the needs of the environment but on an unexamined addiction to profit. In short, we're conducting an experiment on ourselves and on the planet based on the absurd hypothesis that production, consumption, and national boundaries are more important than people.

The myth that is spread by the media is that we're each a competing speck in a hostile, competing universe. If you're lucky, you're a happy speck with a prestigious job in a prosperous speck of a country. If you're not, you're an unhappy speck and you should acquire what it takes to become a happy one, and to do that you need to have more things, experience more sensations, have more fun, and become rich, powerful, or famous.

These ideas are reinforced constantly, so the question is, what do we do about that? We need another source of information in which to immerse ourselves. I'm not suggesting that we turn off the television and never turn it on again. That's really not the answer. The answer is to make room in our lives for another view of what it means to be human. One of the places that alternate view comes from is nature. Take a walk in the morning before you go to work and another after you get home. See how the light changes with the seasons. See how the sun moves in the heavens. Feel how the temperatures change. It's enormously reassuring living in the rhythm of nature. It's reassuring, it's nurturing, and it tells us something about what it is to be human and what life really is.

We're an inextricable part of the matrix of life. Inextricable. No man is an island. Any man's death, any man's degradation diminishes me. I can't hurt you without hurting myself. Spiritual practice tells us that, but in day-to-day life we tend to forget. So try to get a more reliable source of information. Nature is one place to do that. It doesn't have to be much—a little gardening or walking at the same time every day.

The other thing, of course, is meditation because there's a source of light and truth that we all carry inside. If we can take time to step away from all this incoming stimuli, sit down, quiet the body, calm the breath, still the mind, and turn the mind away from the constant thinking, the nature of reality starts to present itself to us on its own terms. It's a very different reality from what we live in every day. It takes a while in meditation to get a direct experience of that, but even the act of moving toward it changes us. From that point we change the world. We have the power to create our own reality. It starts with each of us individually creating our own reality and then it moves out from there to include a collective shift in consciousness.

Spirituality in the Workplace

Jatin DeSai

Jatin Desai is managing partner of DeSai learning, a unique and innovative provider of corporate human resources, strategic leadership, and management education whose client list includes Fortune 10, 100, and 1000 companies. His company's business model creates a unique company culture based on human values, which enhances the quality of work life and the community as well as the bottom line. A graduate of the University of Connecticut, DeSai is also executive director of Prasanthi Center, a community service and education center focusing on education, selfless service, and spirtual leadership in Hartford, Conneticut.

EVERY INDIVIDUAL IS A SPIRITUAL BEING first and foremost. Although many of us spend eight to ten hours a day at work—most of our waking life, in fact—spirituality is taboo in most businesses. The desire to bring spirituality into the workplace, where I believe we need it more than anywhere else, has been my calling for the last ten years.

I happen to be a businessman, an executive, the leader of a company, a mentor, and vendor of services to Fortune 500 companies. At the same time, I've been fortunate enough to have had a spiritual upbringing from a very early age. There was a point in my life, probably about ten or fifteen years ago, when I realized that I had successfully run multiple businesses, yet the values and the spiritual foundation of my youth were not visible in my day-to-day thoughts, words, or deeds. Bridging the gap between worldly success and a lack of spiritual success became my focus. I set out to make work a spiritual arena, a spiritual playground; it wasn't about money any longer. It was about peace and happiness.

I vividly remember how it all began. I sat down in front of my altar at home. It was a Thursday. In Hindu tradition, Thursday is an auspicious day. It is a Guru Day. So on Thursdays I would sit in front of my guru, Satya Sai Baba. After months of reading and reflecting on how to bring spirituality to work, inspiration struck. I started writing down ideas for managing my business. My goal was not just to enhance my personal practice at work but also to create an environment where my employees and customers could connect with themselves and with one another on a deeper level. I came up with a ten-year plan for all the things I wanted to do professionally. Ultimately I wanted to create a business that would not be called a business at all but rather a spiritual sanctuary in a business building. That was the vision.

After developing my ideas, I called a company meeting and announced the inauguration of the Spirit at Work program. Even before this announcement, my employees thought I was kind of crazy. Because I often go to India, they thought that this was some idea I had brought back from India. I explained to them that the Spirit at Work program would have three components: voluntary study circles, community service, and a wisdom library.

The voluntary study circles are held weekly and facilitated by anyone in the company on the topic of his or her choice—as long as it is not related to work. That's the only rule. Every Wednesday a group gets together for about an hour and somebody in the company facilitates a presentation. One employee spoke on Reiki. Another taught a yoga class. We brought in a professional who taught us how to breathe correctly. Many of my colleagues were amazed by the changes in themselves and in the company. One day we had somebody who feels spiritual presence in her hobby, making clay pots. So she brought in clay and everybody sat in a big conference room and made clay pottery. She brought back the fired pieces the next week, and it was an opportunity to reconnect.

The second component of the Spirit at Work program is community service. Among other initiatives, we've adopted an elementary school—and by "we" I mean not just the employees but also our customers. So we've extended our family and we're working on an elementary school. It's a Title 1 school in need of all sorts of things, from bus passes to toothbrushes for the kids who share one toothbrush in a family. Along with the material assistance, we also provide human values education as a part of the school's character-development program. We help them organize field trips, health fairs, and all sorts of other activities. Primarily our role as businesspeople is to be coordinators because the wonderful thing about this country is that all of these resources are already here.

> We cannot change the world or accomplish anything external until we first commit to being our own spiritual leader.

The third component of the Spirit at Work program is a small wisdom library. Employees can borrow books, videos, and audiotapes. They can donate things; they can take things home. There's no check-in/check-out. It's all on a trust system. For my company, the Spirit at Work program is a way to build that kind of environment for all employees who choose to participate.

In our actual work—that is, the work we get paid to do—we provide education to corporations, anything from leadership management to human-resource strategies to organizational development work to basic training services.

There is a formula that we use for all aspects of that work: Performance is equal to potential minus interferences. If I were to substitute the words *spiritual progress* for *performance*, people would think I'm nuts. So I stick with *performance*.

We begin with the premise that potential is already inherent in our clients' businesses. Rather than focus on potential, we help individual employees, teams, and the whole company remove interferences. With our company philosophy, we don't need salespeople. We allow the divine blessings to send the customers to us. And they come. Similarly, the types of people who join the organization as employees are naturally highly connected to the spiritual side of themselves and the world. They get it. We have executives who could have made much more money elsewhere but have opted to leave that world behind to work in a place where they feel their own presence.

So the foundation of this new culture is as follows: Let God manifest what needs to be manifested for the company and everyone here. That's the morning prayer. That's the morning quiet time and that is how the workday begins for me. Therefore it's easy to see these connections or occasionally the lack of them when dealing with a customer. If I am not making that connection with a customer, I just say so upfront. In that case, to work together would be a waste of my time and a waste of their time. Time is the most precious gift in the human body. We don't want to waste it. That's part of being spiritually alive.

If I were to hold up a mala and ask a ten-year-old what it is, what do you think he'd say? Beads. A necklace. If I were to ask a spiritual aspirant, she would say it's a mala. A small shop owner in the foothills of the Himalayan villages would say it's a mala. A saint in the Himalayas might say it's a tool to achieve peace or a reminder of God. A cotton manufacturer would say that's a two-millimeter thread with 108 little beads on it. Definitions vary, though the object remains the same.

The Sacred Link is like that. It has different perspectives. In my view, the Sacred Link can be lived through yoga, through business, through the healing professions, and so on. Each of these disciplines is like an individual bead in a mala. I come from the business bead so I look at the Sacred Link from that perspective. Others come from a health background and look at the link from that perspective.

In order to immerse ourselves in the philosophy of the Sacred Link, we need to be open to looking at it from all the other perspectives. We can't do that without first opening our hearts. We must find out how to do that. We cannot change the world or accomplish anything external until we first commit to being our own spiritual leader. It's not enough to be successful in the world because the measurements of success are well defined and ultimately unfulfilling. We must commit to being spiritually successful. We can't do that from just one bead. There's so much more to learn.

> When we study the teachings of the Himalayan masters and incorporate them into our own lives, we start to live with real purpose and come to feel the touch of the divine in everything we do.

The sooner we see the Sacred Link from multiple perspectives, the sooner we'll be able to live out the full potential of our being. One opportunity to practice that is at work. This doesn't mean you don't practice anywhere else, but for me, as a businessman, it's been very challenging to practice any sort of dharma activity, even quieting the mind, at work.

Practically speaking, you must do a few things in order to begin that self-commitment to become an active participant in the Sacred Link or any other spiritual practice. The first step in the thousand steps that we're going to take in propagating the Sacred Link is to define our own spirituality. That's the first step in being a disciplined inquirer of our own selves.

Everyone has a different definition of spirituality and a different readiness to set out on the inner journey and make a commitment to practice. At the same time, it's like the beads. For me, spirituality is about awareness. It's about awareness that there is a supreme consciousness, that there's a big Self, not the little self that's me.

Of course, we don't have a balanced scorecard and we don't have performance reviews to measure how well we're doing on our spiritual journey, so if we're serious about the journey, we need to be disciplined about it. How we measure progress in our spiritual journey is really up to us. For me, the test of positive progress in my spiritual journey is an increase in compassion. It's having compassion even in cases where you normally would not feel it—in the words or actions of the angriest person, for example. If you can feel compassion for that person, you have advanced on your spiritual journey.

So I think the first step on the path to a spiritual life is to come up with a personal definition of spirituality. The second step is to have a spiritual view of life. That means we have to stop saying that we cannot integrate spirituality in the many other roles that we play: mother, father, sister, brother, manager. I'm not aware of any rule that says you can't integrate spirituality at work.

The third step is to have spiritual purpose, principles, and values. In my case, I have benefited from the enormous legacy that has been passed down to us from the

Himalayan masters. When we study their teachings and incorporate them into our own lives, we start to live with real purpose and come to feel the touch of the divine in everything we do. Only then can we spread the message of the Sacred Link.

First be, then do, and then tell. That's spiritual leadership. I hope you all will join me on this undertaking, the most important one of your career.

Discovering the Sacred Within

Rod   Stryker

Rod Stryker, one of the pre-eminent yoga and meditation teachers in the United States, has taught tantra, meditation, and hatha yoga for more than twenty-five years and continues to lead teacher-training programs and workshops throughout the world. He is the founder of Para Yoga and the author of *The Four Desires,* and has released a series of CDs on meditation and hatha yoga practice. He is also a frequent contributor to *Yoga + Joyful Living* magazine and a board member of the Himalayan Institute.

While Stryker's many years of committed asana practice have made him a master at teaching postures, he is at his best when sharing his insights on more subtle aspects of yogic self-transformation, ranging from meditation to dealing with family issues. He is also one of a very few yoga teachers who can articulate an authentic experience of the tantric tradition.

MY FIRST TEACHER, WHO WAS A SENIOR DISCIPLE of Swami Agehanada Bharti, used to quote a student of Einstein's who said that the theory of relativity was a concept so profound and all-encompassing that at the time Einstein was alive, only seven people understood it completely. They were seven of Einstein's closest disciples. His point was that to this day that no more than those seven will fully understand that knowledge. In a way, tantra is the same. It's so vast and all-inclusive, so sublime and intricate in so many ways that very few people can really hope to capture its full meaning and spirit. Tantra has added so much to my life, and to the extent to which I've stepped into the wisdom of tantra, I am excited to discuss the significance of it within the context of the Sacred Link® vision, which honors the sacred within us all.

Let's begin by laying out a few basic core ideas. Tantra contends that each of us is born at a certain time, under certain conditions. If you have more of a Western psychological mind-set, you think of those conditions not as the influence of past lives or of the stars or of the implication of the planets at any given time, but rather as conditions relating to our parents or the culture that we grew up in or just timing. We were all born into and exist within conditions unique to each of us as individuals, and those conditions have placed certain limits on our abilities, our perceptions, our relationship to ourselves or others. Tantra is the science to overcome those limitations. In the simplest terms, that's what tantra is about.

Tantra, it might surprise some, is a science. One of the meanings of the word *tantra* is "treatise," and that accurately describes it as a massive body of knowledge. It doesn't ask you to spend endless hours and years studying books on the subject. Rather, tantra is by its very nature practical. Tantra means that when you do a certain thing (an action or practice), it spontaneously gives rise to a higher level of awareness or a greater sense of freedom. When you do a tantric technique, it automatically produces a positive effect, a spontaneous effect, regardless of your beliefs. That is, by nature, what makes it tantric.

If you go to the oldest, most influential, most pure yoga text, the *Yoga Sutra* by Patanjali, you'll find it's full of tantric practices. The third chapter consists almost entirely of tantric practices. In the first chapter, the thirty-sixth sutra talks about meditating on a light in the heart that's beyond all sorrow. That's a tantric practice, a practice of joining with some resource that lies beyond. Tantra and yoga share many principles, but in recent times, the two traditions have been dissociated. That separation is a false one, how- ' ever. My teachers taught me that yoga was about peace;

yoga was about transformation; yoga was about transforming oneself and one's world. We did our sadhana, our practice, to create internal changes so that our relationship with the world would be transformed. That message has not stood up very well in today's yoga community, where yoga is often seen merely as a means of stress reduction, or exercise. The idea of tantra has also been distorted and, in the public's mind, is now often believed to involve taking your clothes off. It is my hope that there will be a reawakening and a revival of the real power of these traditions.

Awakening to the Subtle Realm

In *Living with the Himalayan Masters,* Swami Rama writes, "In the depth of silence is hidden the source of love." To what extent do we find silence in our lives? Tantra and yoga together allow us to access the world of silence and the extraordinary knowledge it can impart to us. Perhaps what makes tantra a unique spiritual system is its suggestion that our experience of life is shaped not only by the mind, not only by our culture, our parents, our friends, the time, the decade, or the era that we live within. But it's actually dictated by our pranic landscape—by our energy. Tantric visionaries, or rishis, were able to look into the map of the subtle body, the pranic body. To begin to discover the source of love, we must plumb the depths of silence and discover what lies there.

This exploration, which is the beginning of self-mastery, is different from the psychological approach to self-understanding and self-knowledge, as it is commonly understood in the Western world. Our experience of life is not only the way we see it but also what we do within it, what we imagine is possible. It's actually shaped not just by our perception but also by our energy. By becoming aware of the content of your mind (and I use that term to allude not only to our memory, ego, and psychological makeup—the Western conception of mind—but also to include the totality of experiences from this life and previous lives), you can begin to transform your energy. This awakening to the subtle realm is what tantra yoga is all about.

Swami Satchidananda Saraswati, an astute and accomplished yoga master has said, "When you develop true sensitivity, the world will be an open book to you, revealing on each page new secrets and wonderful knowledge." He was talking about the world of prana, the world of energy. All the great sages tried to impress upon us that the world we see is barely a tip of the iceberg of existence. Barely a tip. Although it's not visible, prana is everywhere, animating everything—known and unknown. Everything that we see, hear, taste, touch, smell, and sense is animated by prana. How hard is it to access? The simple principle is that the more quiet your mind is, the easier it is to access prana. And the more often you access it, the easier it is to get your mind quiet.

The great mechanism to connect to this field of prana, which then gradually increases our sensitivity and our transformational potential, is not your breath but your mind. Your mind's ability to connect to these subtle fields is perhaps its greatest gift. The pranic body in Western mysticism is called the etheric body. The etheric body's one main role from the tantric point of view is to access the quality of liveliness, the quality of vitality that can dissipate the negative effects of wrong living. The role of the pranic body or etheric body is to reduce the impact of our thoughts, emotions, unhealthy diet, and wrong living on the physical body so that we can sustain it, not indefinitely, but for the time that we have life, sustain it so that we can be a vital, creative force.

Well, how do we access the subtle body? It's not as complicated or as lofty as it begins to sound. It's called imagination. Imagination and visualization. When I imagine that there is, let's say, a field of light around my body, is it strictly imaginary? Is it only in my mind? No. That pranic realm is in the mind, in the body, and beyond. So as soon as the mind begins to turn toward some feeling or image related to these subtle realms, one is automatically relating to them.

What follows is a little practice that I think is useful. This technique relates to the theme of Sacred Link. As I said earlier, to a great extent, yoga has been used only for self-improvement—to make our bodies feel better, to be healthier, to feel less stress. What we've lost is the idea that when I think of another and extend compassion to another, I improve myself. When I help another person, we become literally inseparable.

A Tantric Meditation on Love

This practice uses the mind to access the subtle body. It begins with the idea of using intention to help others. If you are interested in helping or healing someone, what I would suggest is that you don't use yourself. Instead rely on the forces of nature. Nature has unlimited resources, whereas our own individual resources are limited. So the first step of this practice involves strengthening and filling your own reservoir of peace. The second step is learning to take that feeling and send it to another.

What we're really talking about is moving love. Unconditional love. And that means you may not know exactly how and what is supposed to happen to the person as a result of this infusion of love. You don't know and you shouldn't impose it. In other words, you might find that you have a predisposition to what that person needs or should become. But that really isn't unconditional love. In this offering, we allow the wisdom of love itself to speak through and to the person.

So just take a moment and think about someone who needs healing or love or wellness. It could be a person or a whole community. It could be someone at home or someone that you know is sick. To begin, sit up tall and close your eyes. Make yourself very comfortable. Soften your shoulders, your jaw, and your lips. And now without moving anything, just feel the feeling of a smile. I'm not asking you to change your expression. Just feel the wave, the overflowing of joy and beauty that is the force behind a gentle smile. Now feel that same feeling surround the physical heart. Feel the heart smiling. Feel the wave of beauty and bliss blossoming in your physical heart. Now see it in the lungs and feel it in the lungs—the feeling of a smile. If you have any particular organ that is suffering from discomfort or disease, see the smile in that individual organ or see it in the totality of internal organs—digestive, reproductive, purificatory (the liver and the kidneys). Now even feel the smile in both legs, both arms. See if you can just jump to that feeling of the smile. Allow the body to relax and feel the unfoldment of the natural state of beauty and bliss, of joy. Feel your entire body as one giant smile. From the head to the toes to the tips of the fingers, feel the smile.

Clinical studies have shown that when we feel love, our immune system is strengthened. The body heals more

> Be a force of love in which you are able to receive it as well as live it as well as give it.

quickly. We age more slowly. When we are stressed and have worries, the opposite unfolds. As you become aware of your whole body, you might notice that the smile is bigger than your form. It means that you are connecting to some field bigger than form, something more transcendent. From a foundation of peace you can now offer peace and wellness to others, not so much by giving away what little peace you may know in your own life but rather drawing upon the limitless ocean of peace and healing and strength. Bring your awareness to the area behind your navel, in your spine. As you breathe in, softly draw the feeling of peace and light up the spine. The breath is very subtle. It's not forced. As you breathe out, just feel it softly release out the top of the head, creating a feeling above your head of a profound sense of peace. As you inhale, the sensation rises through your spine. As you exhale, peace unfolds out the top of the head. There's an amorphous sphere of peace above you, like a cloud. If you like, as you inhale you can say or hear the sound *ah-ooo.* And as you exhale, the sound *mmmm.* Inhale *ah-ooo*, exhale *mmmm.* Repeat three more times.

Now we'll change the practice slightly. The first part is the same, moving from the navel up the spine. But as you exhale, move that energy through the throat. On the inhale, the sound is *shan.* On the exhale the sound is *ti. Shanti,* of course, is the Sanskrti word meaning "peace." *Om* is the sound of the Universal, the Absolute, the Boundless. Now feel this soft movement purifying the throat. The breath is soft. It's effortless. Continue three or four more times: *shan* on the inhale, *ti* on the exhale. Feel that you are literally connecting with the stream of peace, the stream of universal healing.

When you're ready, move to the final stage of the practice. Picture the person, the environment, the people, the country, the culture, the community, or the place where you are sending peace. Channel peace toward wellness, healing, and love. Back at the space behind the navel, draw this feeling of peace up the spine to the third eye center, the middle of the brain. As you exhale, project it out your third eye. If you are sending peace to an individual, it's into the heart center. If it is to a situation, see it pervade the entire environment.

The mantra now is *Om* on the inhale, *shanti* on the exhale. Within a few minutes you may feel a gentle sense that love is being received, absorbed. And we do this unconditionally with no preconception about what needs to happen. Abandon your own self-interests, expectations, and attachments. Gradually feel the dawning of more love for this person, place, or thing—healing and vibrant, strong and flooded with unconditional love. You may even feel that you are uplifted as the recipient is uplifted. Now see or feel that person surrounded by love. In your own heart wish him or her the very best. And then gently come back to your body and to your breath. Inhale slowly and exhale slowly, then gently lower your chin and gradually reopen your eyes, looking down at a point on the floor in front of you as you bring your attention back to the room.

If you practice this meditation, you will find that changes start to happen—sometimes instantaneously. I've certainly seen that in my own life and in the experience of my students who've done this practice.

Creating Your Own Sacred Link

If I distill what I learned in the yoga teachings, I see three main themes. The first is fearlessness. Swami Rama spoke about coming to a point in our lives where we live without fear. And to that end I think the tantric tradition offers a rich, rich resource. The death of fear is the awakening of the Sacred Link. I often ask students to look at the lives of such great teachers as Ramakrishna, Swami Rama, Yogananda, Vivekananda, and many others. They were truly living sages but, at some level, they also were men and women who practiced. These great adepts were not isolationists who just sat in *samadhi* eon after eon and refused to enter the world. A sage ultimately becomes a vehicle to expand the greater good. And I believe that the Sacred Link unfolds when fear and self-isolation or self-preoccupation begin to dissipate. We, by nature, become more generous and more inclusive. We try to light other lights, and in the process our own light becomes brighter.

The second key part of the message is *sankalpa shakti*. It means "the power of your resolve." What are you resolved to accomplish in this lifetime? Make an absolute commitment to becoming self-realized and using that self-realization to help others. Sankalpa shakti ties in to the third message, which, as I see it, is the culmination of these practices. And it's also what my first teacher taught me. As complex as tantra is, as vast as this science is, it culminates in learning to love, to give, to be more generous and more expansive in our love. We should not aim to be martyrs of love—people who just give and give and give. Nor should we be people who are on the other side, just wanting to receive. Be the loving. Be a force of love in which you are able to receive it as well as live it as well as give it.

> To begin to discover the source of love, we must plumb the depths of silence and discover what lies there.

I'd like to close with an image from one of the Upanishads: Each of us is like an unlit match. All of the ingredients for that match are in the match from the moment it is created. Does it get lit? It's a question of whether there is some catalyst. Let your practice be the catalyst, the process that awakens the flame in your match.

The Upanishad says: "He who chooses the Infinite is chosen by the Infinite." Choose to merge with the Infinite. She will choose to merge with you. Don't wait. Don't put it off. Don't think it is someone else's business and you will get the breadcrumbs of their experience. Begin the journey. *He who chooses the Infinite is chosen by the Infinite.*

Prescription for Radiant Living

Carrie Demers, M.D.

Dr. Demers is the director of the Himalayan Institute's Center for Health and Healing. As a newly minted M.D. doing her residency in Chicago, Dr. Demers discovered a disconcerting fact: her medical training had prepared her to deal with health emergencies, but she didn't know how to help her patients stay well. So she turned to complementary medicine and the holistic health model of ayurveda, applying them to her own life as well as those of her patients. In her role as director of the Center for Health and Healing, Dr. Demers designs individualized wellness programs, drawing on her knowledge of Western internal medicine, traditional approaches to health, and the therapeutic benefits of hatha yoga.

AYURVEDA IS AN INCREDIBLE SYSTEM of disease treatment. But at its heart it is really a system of wellness, of disease prevention. This essay will offer some practical information for maintaining vitality and enhancing radiance. Those qualities are the fruits of your inner fire. By using some of the tools described below, you can build that fire to sustain your physical, mental, and spiritual well-being.

In Sanskrit fire is *agni*. In Ayurveda, fire is usually thought of as a digestive fire—the fire that lives in your belly and digests your food. But agni is actually much more than that. Agni gives you immune strength. It gives you vitality and energy. Mental clarity and intelligence also come out from that fire.

In Ayurveda, there is a term for that radiance that people have when they're vibrantly healthy: *ojas*. Ojas is our vital sap, our radiant energy. It's the end product of digestion.

From digestion, a hierarchy of tissues arises. Each tissue nourishes the next one, starting from most gross and most abundant and moving to the densest tissues in our bodies. So you eat a meal and it nourishes your plasma; your plasma nourishes your blood; your blood nourishes your muscles; your muscles nourish the fat; fat nourishes your bones; bones nourish your bone marrow, which includes the nervous system inside bony cavities. Your bone marrow nourishes your sexual organs. Finally, the smallest, most potent parts of you actually nourish ojas. The whole process of digestion—taking what's nourishing from the food you eat and passing out the waste—happens at every level and gets more and more subtle, nourishing you at a deeper and deeper level. The end product is ojas.

We age because we lose ojas. We're all born with a measure of prenatal ojas. Kids are little bundles of ojas. I have a three-year-old who is full of juice. He's squishy, he drools, his nose runs. That juice is part of ojas. So is the capacity for spontaneous unconditional love. Kids are just little packets of love. They don't know any better. That's why we're so in awe of babies and toddlers. It's God coming through. They haven't boxed themselves into rules or societal norms yet. When I leave, my three-year-old gives me two kisses in this ear and two kisses on this cheek. He's just a little lovebug.

We have lots of resilience as children. As young adults, we run wild and bungee-jump and stay up all night for weeks at a time. Maybe we do drugs and have wild sex. In other words, we throw away ojas. For some of us, it deteriorates quickly. Maybe we are given less or we burn it up faster. For others, the process is more gradual.

In Ayurveda, there's a term for the cause of disease: *prajna aparadha*. It means "crimes against wisdom." It means we do what we know we shouldn't do. We go out without a hat. We're full but we overeat anyway. We know something really doesn't serve us, but we're pulled by our desires and so we do it anyway. And the really lovely thing is that the Sanskrit word for immunity means "forgiveness of the disease." The concept is quite poetic: Our immunity, our ability to fight off illness is forgiveness for all the things we've done; our body has compassion on our weak will or on our lack of self-control.

As we run out of that early supply of ojas, we have to be responsible and make our own ojas so that we have this vital sap to keep us strong. Not only does ojas give us radiance—vibrant physical health—there is actually a peace and a harmony and a loving nature that comes from ojas. Think of the images of saints and sages. They have halos. Mother Mary has a halo. According to Ayurveda that halo is a sign of abundant ojas.

How do we make ojas? First, we need to stoke the fire. The fire lives at our solar plexus. Your sun in the form of fire lives at your solar plexus. Right where your ribs come down above your navel, that's where your stomach meets the first part of your intestine, called the duodenum. Biologically, that's where we have the most enzymatic fire. Your stomach acid meets your bile and your pancreatic juice right there. People get duodenal ulcers when there's so much enzymatic activity devouring them that they actually erode their mucosal membrane.

Good fuel isn't just what you take in through your mouth. It's also what you consume through your senses and your relationships. By turning our attention inward in meditation, we connect to a feeling of deep peace and rediscover our loving nature.

We want to keep this fire strong, but not so aggressive that it attacks us. To do that we must stoke that fire. The simplest way to stoke this fire is to breathe diaphragmatically. The diaphragm is a muscle shaped like an upward-facing dome, and the lungs are stuck to the top of it. And as you inhale, your diaphragm contracts down right over your solar plexus, pulling your lungs down so they inflate all the way to the bottom. As you exhale, your diaphragm pops back up and your lungs collapse. The action of the diaphragm going up and down fans your solar plexus.

To improve your digestion, simply pause for a few minutes before you eat and breathe deeply and slowly. Support that fire. Even that simple addition to your usual routine can help your agni. Then, of course, yoga practice includes pranayama. Any one of the vigorous breathing practices, such as *kapalabhati* or *bhastrika,* fans the fire. If you do those practices for a minute or two, you really feel the heat rise in your body. You're increasing that solar plexus fire. That's the first thing. Stoke the fire.

The other way to make ojas is with exercise. When you build heat in your body, you support your fire. The exercise could be just walking, or it could be stomach crunches and leg lifts that work the abdominal muscles. Some people think crunches are hard. But the truth is they're not hard if you tell yourself that all you need to do is five a day. Do five a day and then do seven a day, then do nine a day, and then do eleven a day. Every week go up by two. Give a little bit of attention to this part of your body every day.

Agni sara is another excellent practice that energizes the solar plexus area. Swami Rama, the founder of the Himalayan Institute, used to say to people, "If you do no other asana practice, at least do agni sara." Why is it so important? It moves the congestion that lives in our bellies.

We're a culture that's taught to suck in our stomachs and walk around with our bellies held static, and so we breathe up in our chests. Our bellies tend to get stagnant and we become susceptible to such digestive problems as constipation and diverticulitis. Ovarian cysts, uterine fibroids, prostate hypertrophy—all this stuff lives in the pelvic area because we don't move it. If things stagnate they're bound to get diseased.

Agni sara energizes that stagnant area. It moves the energy in the lower three chakras. The first three chakras govern security, fear, passion, anger, control, and self-esteem. So you're moving stuck energy from your heart, from your throat, from your higher energy centers upward so you can use it in the world. Agni sara is very helpful on a physical as well as on a more subtle level.

Instead of dissipating our energy, agni sara trains us to use and control energy in the body, to retain it and even magnify the energy in our system. As a physician in Wisconsin, I used to do house calls to elderly patients. I was a total novice, a new yoga student, but I began to see a void in the solar plexus area of these old, homebound people. There was a slouching over. They had pouched bellies and sometimes became incontinent. Their energy was dissipating. Agni sara is a practice to make you continent, to make you contain, make you condense, to help hold you together. That's why I think Swami Rama said, "If you do nothing else, do agni sara." It's so important for your energy, your vitality, your health, and your clarity of mind.

The first step toward radiance is to fan the fire through breathing, exercise, and asana practice. The second step is to keep the fire strong by clearing away any burden or toxins that could weaken that fire. If you were at a campfire and you put a big, heavy, wet log on top of the fire, you might just smother the flames. We do this in our lives.

We burden ourselves. Sometimes it's with food—the Thanksgiving meal is a good example. After we overeat, we feel tired. We feel heavy. That's a sign that we've just smothered our ability to digest.

The Basics of Agni Sara

Stand with your feet slightly wider than hip width apart. Keeping the spine straight, bend the knees slightly and rest your hands on your thighs. The weight of the torso rests on the arms. As you exhale, squeeze your navel toward your spine. Really accentuate the exhale. As you inhale, let your belly relax. Repeat five to ten times.

Once you have mastered the abdominal squeeze, you may choose to add *mula bandha*, the root lock. This entails contracting and lifting the muscles of the pelvic floor. For women, the sensation is similar to Kegel exercises; you squeeze up through the vaginal barrel. For men, the focus is on the perineum, the area between the anus and the genitals. On the exhale, contract the muscles of the pelvic floor, drawing them up and in as you squeeze your navel toward your spine. On the inhale, gradually release the pelvic floor as you allow your abdomen to soften.

Repeat five to ten times. Agni sara is best performed on an empty stomach.

Agni digests not just food but also the air we breathe and the mental and emotional impressions that we take in throughout our lives. Agni's job is to take what's useful and pass out the waste. If we're not passing out the waste, the body and mind are burdened. Our fire is smothered.

So the next thing that you have to do to keep your fire strong is to get rid of the waste. It's really quite simple. You have four main detoxification organs in your body that are routes for eliminating waste: your bowels, your bladder and your kidneys, your skin (through sweat), and your lungs. Actually, your tongue and your sinuses can also be used to expel toxins. So be mindful of that. Have a bowel movement every day. Give yourself an opportunity to be regular. Drink enough fluid. Eat enough fiber and get some exercise. All these things help your body get rid of that solid waste. Drink enough water. What's enough? I tell people their urine should be pale yellow or colorless. You should be able to read newsprint through it. That's a sign that you're drinking enough fluid to flush your kidneys. For some people, that might be six glasses a day. For others, it might be a gallon a day. It depends on the person. Pay attention to your body.

Pay attention not just to your spiritual self but also to your physical self. What affects you? What color is your urine? What's the quality of your stool? What's the quality of your sweat? These details are actually interesting if you pay attention. You need to sweat. So go out there and work out four or five times a week so that you break a sweat. That's another way for your body to get rid of toxins.

And finally, you want to breathe. We breathe somewhere between twelve and fifteen times a minute. Modern doctors think that up to twenty breaths a minute is normal, but twenty is much too fast. Fast breathing is shallow and doesn't properly clear the lungs. Other bad breathing habits, like holding our breath, hold in volatile wastes and make us feel bad.

So attend to those four organs in your body: the lungs,

the skin, the bowels, and the bladder. Actually, in Ayurveda, we say you can do other things, such as a nasal wash with the Neti Pot™ and tongue scraping. It's fabulous to wash the sinuses every day. You wash out all the gunk you've breathed in. You can prevent sinus infections and alleviate allergies. If you scrape your tongue every morning with a spoon or a tongue scraper, you create a little less burden on your body by getting rid of some toxins. You can also learn about the state of your health. Tongue scraping is like the toxin meter. There's an Ayurvedic word for the toxins in the body: *ama*. It means "indigestible stuff." Ama is visible on the tongue. Sometimes you go a whole week with practically nothing on your tongue. Your body's burning clean. And some weeks you might think, Yuck. There's something like cream cheese on my tongue scraper. What's happening? Tongue scraping is like biofeedback. How am I eating? How am I exercising? What's my stress level? What's dampening my agni? Why am I struggling and making more ama instead of ojas?

So we fan the fire with breath and exercise and clean out the toxins. The third thing is to eat good food. You must give your fire good fuel to burn. Even if you do yoga and practice agni sara, you won't build ojas if you eat junk fast food every day. We all know what good fuel is—and what it isn't. Don't eat chemicals; don't eat hydrogenated oils. Those are the most common pitfalls. Almost all processed foods in the grocery store—the crackers, the cookies—contain hydrogenated or partially hydrogenated oils, and they're toxic.

White sugar, white flour, and all those highly refined carbohydrates can also cause damage to our bodies. (The probable reason why people who go on the Atkins diet actually improve their cholesterol profile is that they stop eating white flour and white sugar and that's what makes the cholesterol better.) Ideally, you eat sugars that are natural—dried fruit or succanat, which is dried cane juice. Maple syrup, rice syrup, and barley malt are natural sweeteners that are less taxing on the body than the more refined, concentrated products. Raw honey is good as long as you don't cook with it. Stevia is a great herbal sweetener.

Some people advocate raw food because it is packed with enzymes and vitamins and nutrients. But you have to be able to extract those nutrients. If your agni isn't strong, raw food will upset your stomach and make you bloated. When you cook food, you break down the cell walls of the plant, making eating it easier to assimilate. There's no one right way. It's all about experimentation. Direct experience is the best information. If you eat raw food and feel good, if your agni is happy, if your food moves through you well, and if you feel enlivened by it—great. But if you eat in a way that makes you feel burdened or congested or tired or nauseated, it's time to find something else.

Good fuel isn't just what you take in through your mouth. It's also what you consume through your senses and your relationships. Ask yourself, am I overusing my senses? Am I sitting at the computer eight hours a day? Do I have my Walkman on my head for ten hours a day? How am I choosing to feed my senses? It's important to spend some time attending to your inner world. Meditate, pray, sing, paint—do whatever works to connect to that deep place inside you, the place that gives you the feeling that all is right with the world. Our agni, the fire that's inside of us, is our link to that other fire, the divine light in and around us. By giving our senses a daily break from information and stimuli and by turning our attention inward in meditation, we can connect to a feeling of deep peace and rediscover our loving nature. That is what I wish for all the readers of this book—vibrant physical health coupled with an awareness of our true nature and inner harmony.

Healing the Heart

Stephen Nezezon, M.D.

Dr. Stephen Nezezon, a board-certified psychiatrist with a subspecialty in addiction psychiatry, is on the faculty of the Himalayan Institute. He has received nationally recognized certification in biofeedback, acupuncture, and homeopathy, and has been interviewed by *Prevention* and *Natural Health* magazines as well as by the Fox Network. Dr. Nezezon's private practice emphasizes integrative medicine, combining Western allopathic methods with nutritional and herbal treatments, homeopathy, yoga, and ayurveda.

SWAMI RAMA USED TO SAY THAT THE essence of life is relationship. If we relate properly to all the people and all the elements in our life, we're happy. But if we have imbalances in those relationships internally and externally, we disturb our ease and thus, to borrow Swami Satchidananda's wordplay, we become "dis-eased." We become diseased.

In my psychiatry practice, I see many forms of emotional heart disease. There is the four-year-old boy whose parents divorced when he was two; every week he sends his father a drawing or message but he hasn't received a single reply in two years. That's emotional heart disease. There are patients dealing with the death of a spouse, a divorce after fifty years of marriage, a sudden decline in health, or the transition to an assisted living center. Those are all examples of emotional heart disease.

Even without such major upheavals, emotional heart disease can occur. When we rent out space in our heart, as one author put it, to pain and resentment and cynicism, to hostility and envy and jealousy, we cannot feel the love of the Divine or our love for ourselves or the love that others have for us. When that happens, heart disease can set in— emotional and physical heart disease.

Two researchers, Dr. Red Williams and Dr. Virginia Williams, have devoted themselves to looking at the connection between negative emotions and physical ailments of the heart. And one of the conclusions of their research was that there's nothing wrong with being most of the things that we usually think of as Type A behavior. You can work hard. You can be passionate about what you do. You can be devoted to a cause. You can give up sleep. You can deprive yourself to achieve your goal as long as you don't become cynical. Why is cynicism so toxic? I think it's like having one foot on the accelerator and one foot on the brakes. A cynic knows he has the answer to all the world's problems, but he's equally sure that nobody's going to listen to him.

Other researchers have shown that when you experience negative emotions, the arteries that feed your heart constrict. If you're sitting in traffic and getting worked up because they're doing construction yet again and you're in a hurry to get somewhere, your blood pressure goes up. Adrenaline is secreted, causing the blood to clot more readily and eventually increasing the risk of heart attack.

What to do in such situations? Well, I once had a meal in Chicago at one of those little restaurants where there were only two people working, two brothers: one waited tables, the other cooked. It was lunchtime and an executive came in and was clearly in a hurry. He placed his order and said he needed it quickly. The waiter replied, "As you can see, my brother is cooking, and there are a couple of orders ahead of yours. But as soon as he is finished, I'll deliver it to you." A minute went by and during that time the customer checked his watch five or six times. Then he called the waiter over and said, "Where's my order?" And the waiter, who was actually a saint in disguise, looked at the man with great kindness and said, "Please, sir, don't disturb yourself." He didn't yell at him and say, "Can't you see my brother is working as fast as he can? Just be quiet for a minute or go across the street to McDonald's if you want to." No. He didn't say that. He just looked at him with great kindness and said, "You know, you're in charge of your life. You can choose to be patient or you can choose to be impatient but it's your choice. You're the ruler of this domain. You are the king of this empire that is you. Rule wisely and you'll have a happy kingdom."

So how do we achieve emotional balance? Let's begin by examining an ancient yogic model that will help us understand who are we and how we operate. The self is understood as comprising five *koshas*, or sheaths, nested one inside another, like the Russian dolls. The outermost sheath is the physical body *(annamaya kosha)*, which is made out of food. Next comes the energetic body *(pranamaya kosha)*. Continuing inward, we reach the mental and emotional body *(manomaya kosha)*. Moving deeper still, we find the sheath of intuition or inner wisdom *(vijnanamaya kosha)*. Finally, the innermost sheath is one of pure bliss *(anandamaya kosha)*. These outer three layers—the physical, the energetic, and the emotional—may or may not be in balance. And if they are not in balance, we can have illness on the physical level, on the energetic level, or on the mental and emotional level.

Fortunately, there are some tools to restore health to the

> We can create the kind of world that is heaven on earth or we can create the kind of hell some of the world is today. We have that power.

physical body, the energetic body, and the mental and emotional body. Physically, what can we do for nutritional heart
disease? Some people say we are what we eat. To some
extent that's true. Our food body is made of what we eat.
And we are swamped with information about what to eat or
what not to eat to keep the heart healthy. Swami Rama used
to take a more practical approach. He said that it doesn't
matter so much what you eat; what matters is the attitude
with which you eat it. People in ancient times and many of
us today still pause for a moment before we eat, and in some
way say thank you to the universe for nurturing us yet again.
And when we pause for a moment to say grace, we move
our attention from the outside world to our inner world. We
get ready to receive the gift of nurturance. It doesn't matter
what you say, what language you say it in, how long it takes.
What matters is that you pause for a moment, silently or
with words, and get ready to receive a gift.

While sustenance is a welcome gift, there are other
offerings that are best refused as far as the heart is concerned. There's an ancient story about the Buddha. One
day he's out begging with one of his new disciples. They go
to a house and knock on the door. The woman who comes
to the door isn't having a great day. She says, "Oh, it's you
again. I can hardly feed my own family and you two look
like you could go out and do an honest day's work. Why are
you preying on poor people like me?" And she scoops up
some dirt, puts it in the Buddha's bowl, and slams the door
in their faces.

The Buddha tips his bowl over, wipes it out, and is
ready to go on. But his student is furious. The Buddha says,
"What's wrong?" The student says, "How could she do
that to you? How could she insult you so? Doesn't it make
you angry?" The Buddha, who could have been working in
that restaurant I mentioned before, says, "Please, my son,

don't disturb yourself." He says, "Think for a moment. If someone wants to give you a gift and you accept it, it belongs to you. But if someone wants to give you a gift and you say no thank you, then it goes back to the person who is giving it to you."

When someone says, "You look beautiful today" or "Have a wonderful day" or "God bless you"—those things are worth accepting. Then they belong to us. But if someone is having a bad day and says, "I don't care about you. Just get out of my way," we can take it to heart and let it upset us and give ourselves a little emotional heart disease. Or we can say, "Oh, let me say a prayer for him. He's having such a bad day." We can create the kind of world that is heaven on earth or we can create the kind of hell some of the world is today. We have that power.

In addition to remedies for physical heart disease, there are also homeopathic medicines that work at the energetic level. I had one patient who was a victim of abuse as a little girl and who held much grief locked up in her heart. There's a remedy in homeopathy for people who do that, who keep all those emotions locked up in their heart. It's called Natrum Muriaticum. I gave it to this woman along with breathing and relaxation exercises and nutrition counseling, and she was able to break down some of the walls around her heart. Her marriage improved significantly, as did her life in general. That's why most of us go into the healing profession. We want to help people break down the walls.

There are other remedies in energy medicine. One of the simplest is a flower essence combination called Rescue Remedy. I've used it many times and never had anything but good results. Rescue Remedy is given for shocks to the system, including the heart—for example, when we lose someone we love. Energy medicines can help to strengthen the energy in our heart or in other areas; they can give us the strength and courage we need to get through those difficult times.

Rescue Remedy helps with the shock and the trauma and the congestion in the mind, in the heart, and in the throat center. At the Himalayan Institute, our pharmacist modified Rescue Remedy by adding oplopanax, a Native American herb that gives you strength and courage to move through a crisis. So those are just a couple of examples of medicines that work on the energetic level. If you want to read more about energy medicine, I highly recommend *Radical Healing,* a wonderful book about integrative medicine by Dr. Rudolph Ballentine, who was my mentor.

In the kosha model, the layer of being beneath prana is manomaya kosha, the mental or emotional body. It is here that the chatter of everyday living goes on: *Did I remember to lock the door when I left the house? I don't think my co-worker likes me.* The mind is constantly turning, and one way to restore balance in our emotional lives is to manage these incessant thoughts so that we have the space to become aware of the deeper layers of our being and the divine spark that resides within each of us.

In 1974 I made my first trip to India and had the good fortune to meet Anandamayi Ma, a sage. I was able to sit in her presence for an hour or so as she was taking questions from the audience. Someone raised a hand and said, "I feel lonely much of the time. Is there anything I can do to help myself?" She said, "Yes. But before I answer your question, I have to tell you that although I've been alone many times in my life, I've never experienced loneliness because as far back as I can remember I was always aware of the presence of my Beloved within, the presence of the Divine. In the company of that one, how can you be lonely?"

On the highest level, that's the solution. If we never forget who we are, we can never be lonely. We have the divine within us; we are finite vessels that hold the infinite.

Three decades after meeting Anandamayi Ma, I returned to India and met another sage. All day long people came and asked for his blessing, and he would bless them and they would go. Some of them would leave an offering in gratitude. Whatever was received was given away five minutes later to someone else who would come and who had nothing. So all day long things came in and all day long things went out.

One of the younger students who was there said, "Sir, I am so impressed with your selflessness. You're just giving, giving, giving. You don't keep anything for yourself." Of course, saints and sages don't need to be praised because they know who they are. They give because that's their nature. They love. They teach. So he said, "No, you shouldn't say that about me. Really, I'm very selfish." She looked shocked and said, "Sir, how can you say that? All day long things came in. All day long things went out. You kept nothing for yourself. How can you say you're selfish?"

He said, "Well, you have to see things from my perspective. You have to understand that I believe there is only one being in the universe. The same one who dwells in my heart dwells in your heart. There is only one Self, one Divine Being. We're just one many, many, many times. So I can't give anything away. I can give it to myself here, or I can give it to myself there, but really I can only give it to myself, so how can I be selfless? I'm selfish. I give it to the same Self. I give it to her

> The mind is constantly turning, and one way to restore balance in our emotional lives is to manage these incessant thoughts so that we have the space to become aware of the deeper layers of our being and the divine spark that resides within each of us.

as myself. I give it to him as myself. It's all myself."

He is right. There is only one Self. My prayer is that someday we all know that. Then we will have achieved our ultimate aim, and then we have truly healed the heart.

Honoring Our Sacrament
with the Natural World

Sandra Anderson

Sandra Anderson, the co-author of the best-selling *Yoga: Mastering the Basics* and two accompanying DVDs, is on the faculty of the Himalayan Institute and a frequent contributor to *Yoga International* magazine (now *Yoga + Joyful Living*). She grew up on the High Plains of Nebraska, where life revolved around the land and the weather. Living close to the rhythms of nature led her to a career in environmental geology. She turned to yoga in the early 1980s and has been a practitioner and teacher ever since, leading teacher-training workshops and seminars nationwide.

FOR YEARS I WORKED IN THE FIELD of environmental cleanup, regulating hazardous waste management and the cleanup of soil and water. After a while it became apparent to me that many environmental problems could not be resolved until we first cleaned up our internal environment. Only then could we make the right decisions about how to manage the external world, the environment, the world of ecology. Now, as a yoga practitioner and teacher, I am in the business of internal environmental cleanup.

It has become increasingly clear to me that as yoga practitioners we must do more than simply transform our bodies and enhance our physical well-being. We must also transform our relationship with our inner self and with our external world. We have to transform our worldview. The situation has become urgent. Our prevailing worldview of nature as a commodity, and of the goal of life to consume that commodity, has resulted not only in the destruction of our climate and the nourishing matrix of the planet but also in disastrous social relationships. The majority of the world's population is struggling with a shortage of the basic necessities for survival, while a small sector of the global economy indulges in a resource feeding frenzy that has destabilized the climate. There is a loss in the stability in the natural world, and we're seeing the results everywhere. Models predicting changes in the climate have been surprisingly accurate to date. The ones that gave us doomsday predictions back in 1990 have been on target so far. So the news is not good.

What's required now is not more of the same but a change in view, a change in perspective, a change in priority, a change in what we value most. We must consider our deeply felt connection with all humanity and redefine "success," "happiness," the goal of life, and most certainly and profoundly, our relationship to the natural world.

If we look back at the traditional yoga literature, we see a different perspective on the natural world and its relation to human beings. Man is seen as part of the natural world, not in competition with it, not in an antagonistic relationship with it, not in a subject/object relationship with it but rather of the same substance as the natural world. In the *Yoga Sutra*, the "bible" of yoga, we encounter the concepts of *purusha* and *prakriti*. Purusha is the Self, that ineffable essence that we might think of as Truth or God or pure consciousness. And then we have prakriti—nature. Prakriti isn't something "out there" in the universe. It isn't a dry intellectual concept. Prakriti is the mountains, the rivers, the rain, the grass growing, and the forces of nature—the essence of nature itself. Prakriti is also our own inherent human nature. And prakriti is permeated with purusha, with consciousness.

The entire natural world is sacred. Of course, this is not

a novel idea. Many indigenous and traditional societies understand this, but we have marginalized them and assigned their wisdom to the categories of "mythology" or amusing stories. And that's exactly where things have gone so terribly wrong not only in the environment but also in our relationships with one another; and between cultures and countries.

This loss of the sacredness of the natural world is, if not the root of our problems, at least a very significant part of the misdirection that we see in our world situation. And it means that even when we make decisions that protect the environment, our actions are based on limited knowledge. We continue studying the natural world just so we can figure out how to control it more. And that might mean that we decide to stop putting carbon dioxide into the atmosphere because if we don't we're going to drown Florida and Manhattan. But it's still a control issue. And it's based on a limited knowledge that's usually falling behind the curve. By the time we figure out that we need to stop putting carbon dioxide into the air and do something about it, much damage is already done. What is missing today is a basic respect and a sense of devotion, of praise, of gratitude, of connection with the forces of nurturance in the universe, the natural world. We would not for a moment think of dumping mercury into the lakes or of throwing our trash onto the side of the road if we had that kind of respect.

When there's a change in our understanding and in our perspective, then the decisions we make about how to live automatically take the environment into account. That's exactly what we see in the spiritual literature related to yoga. In the Puranas for example, anytime there's peace and prosperity in the kingdom it's because the king has established a *dharma,* or rightful action. It's not only that everyone is happy and prosperous but also in the same sentence we are told that all the trees yield fruit, the rains come on time, the seasons follow their natural patterns, the rivers run their course. There is no hunger, no poverty, no disease, no loneliness. It's heaven on earth.

Our mental states are intertwined with the ecological balance in the world. There is no happiness, no well-being, no sense of connectedness and joy in our hearts unless those qualities also exist in the external world. The two things go together in synchrony. This pattern is found over and over again in the scriptures. When Rama was re-established to his rightful place as king of Ayodhya, there was peace and prosperity and everything was right in the world. And there was no disease or old age or hunger. At that time, society was organized in such a way that when a king was righteous, everybody else was too, and the king essentially brought the divine consciousness down to the earthly plane.

Another such king mentioned in the Puranas is Yayati. He instructed his subjects to follow the path of dharma and worship Vishnu, who is a maintaining, stabilizing, nurturing force in the universe. Vishnu often is called upon to rescue things that have gone awry. As a result of worshiping Vishnu, all of Yayati's subjects became righteous. Old age, disease, and sorrow were banished from earth. People stopped dying. Yama, the Lord of Death, had no more work to do and was alarmed. He complained to Indra, the Lord of Heaven, that his occupation was threatened because of Yayati's goodness; the earth had become like heaven. This is a description that we find often in the Puranas.

In the Christian tradition, of course, we have the Garden of Eden. In all of the early traditions there are similar allusions not just to a physical paradise but also to a paradisiacal state of mind. We might want to think about how to move toward such a place from where we are now. And interestingly enough, the scriptures have many descriptions of how things get off track, and what can be done about it.

For example, there is a story in the *Devi Mahatmyam,* which is one of the Puranas—seven hundred verses describing the exploits of the Mother of the Universe. One of the stories is about Shumba and Nishumba, who were very powerful rulers. They ended up with all the good things in the world at that time. They had the most beautiful gems, the finest horses, the best elephants. They had all the riches. They had complete control over the three worlds. Everything was theirs. They had the finest of everything. This is another common theme—the overthrow of the rightful order in the universe. And that starts to sound a little familiar to us as well—people overthrowing the rightful patterns of the natural environment because they have the power to do so.

At that point the beleaguered rightful guardians of the world pray for help. So the gods devised a plan and sent the Mother of the Universe to sit on a mountain in the form of a beautiful woman—Devi. And the servants of Shumba and Nishumba saw this gorgeous jewel among women sitting on the mountain and came back and said to Shumba and Nishumba, "My lords, you have everything else. Here's the most beautiful woman in the world. You have the most beautiful gems. You have the most beautiful horses. You should have the most beautiful woman in the world as well." And they said, "Well, yes, of course. Go and tell her to come to us and we'll give her everything she wants."

The servants went and told her, singing the praises of their lords and saying how wonderful they were and how they would give her everything. And she said, "Alas, I have taken a vow that I will marry only he who defeats me in battle. What a silly thing, but I've done that and so here I am." The servants went back and of course Shumba and

Nishumba were a little bit puffed up because they had the power of the whole world and how dare anyone tell them no. Does this sound familiar?

So they were annoyed and sent their servants back again. This argument went on until finally the lords made a threat: if she didn't come peacefully, they would drag her by her hair, which was the ultimate insult in those days. She said, "What can I do?" They sent out the army, thinking that it would be no problem to overcome just one woman sitting there.

Of course, they didn't realize that she had all the powers of the universe at her disposal. All the rightful lords of the universe came forward to help her. They brought their weapons and bestowed them on her. She and her tiger destroyed the first army in nothing flat. She uttered one mantra of disgust and the army was flattened. Increasingly more powerful generals came forward to try to defeat her, and they were more and more embarrassed and more and more angry because, after all, it was just one beautiful young woman and a tiger. What was the problem? The story goes on and eventually Shumba and Nishumba themselves fight with her and are defeated.

Personally and collectively as a nation, we have the riches of the world. We have all the material things in the world. We have commandeered all the forces of nature to serve us, to serve our small purposes, to serve our personal desires and gratify our senses. It's when we try to ask Devi herself, the force of the universe, to serve our small ego that we run into problems.

In a way, this same scenario is playing out on a world scale, too. And it is happening in the yoga community, just to bring it back down on a more mundane level. We have everything in the West, but we are spiritually hungry. So now we see Devi sitting on the mountain in the Himalayas.

And we have gone to the Himalayas and said, "We have everything in the West. Come live with us. Come be our yoga teacher and serve us because we have everything and we'll give you all the riches." And the problem is, we're asking the Lord of the Universe to serve us instead of offering to serve the Lord of the Universe. So rather than serve the forces of nature, we're demanding that they serve us, according to our petty desires and our limited perspective. And that's where the problem is.

After the defeat of Shumba and Nishumba, there was rejoicing at the return of right thinking in the world and praise for the goddess Devi. In part one hymn of praise to her reads:

> You are the sole substratum of the world.
> You exist in the form of the earth.
> By you who exist in the shape of water all this is gratified.

Again, prakriti is not up there somewhere in the heavens. This divine force is right here in the earth. It's here in the water. It's here in our own hearts. It's here in the world that we're living in. It's here in the natural world. It's not separate from us. It's part of what we are.

> You abide as intelligence in the hearts of all creatures.
> O, Queen of the Universe, you protect the universe.
> As the Self of the universe, you support the universe.
> Those who bow in devotion to you themselves become the refuge of the universe.

What we're looking for is right in front of us, yet somehow we're so disconnected that we don't grasp the sacredness of our daily acts, our daily life, and our daily work.

So how do we return to this sense of sacredness, this

state of paradise? In the Puranas, the descriptions of what needs to happen to establish and maintain rightful order in the world usually involve the notion of sacrifice. Now there's an unpopular word! Let me quickly say that we can think of *yajña* instead, which is a slightly bigger concept that includes the idea of making offerings or oblations, of unconditional giving. The whole universe is essentially based on this notion of giving. The prescription for the current state of affairs, which is described so clearly, is to abandon our selfish desires and serve the greater good, to serve the forces of nature, to serve the world itself, to serve the rightful order in the world.

This is not a foreign concept in our Western tradition. It's just a question of how to implement it. In the scriptures, there is a description of propitiating the forces of nature through fire offerings. That's certainly one possibility. But there are many other ways we can serve in our daily lives. We can start by removing the self-centered motivation in our actions and working for the larger good and well-being of the world rather than our personal interests. That would be one of the first things to do. And we can build awareness of our place in the ecosystem. A famous passage from the *Bhagavad Gita* states:

Beings are born from food.
Food is produced from rain.
And rain is produced from sacrifice, from yajña
And yajña arises from action.

Our lives are supported by food and that food is nourished by the rain. The rain comes from the atmosphere of the clouds, which is itself nourished by our nourishment of it.

In 2003 forty-eight states issued mercury advisories

saying that it wasn't safe to eat the fish from any of the waters in those states. Forty-eight states! Alaska and Wyoming were the only exceptions. Mercury contaminates the surface water everywhere. Where is this mercury coming from? It's coming out of the atmosphere in the rain. And it's going into the atmosphere from the offering of our coal-burning power plants, which spew a stream of toxic metals, including mercury, as well as carbon dioxide and sulfur dioxide into the atmosphere. The rain then washes the metals down onto the soil and from there into the waterways, then into the rivers, streams, and lakes. We're focusing on mercury because it is very toxic in small quantities and it accumulates in fish in a very toxic form. But there are also other metals; sulfur dioxide is the basis for acid rain, and carbon dioxide is a greenhouse gas that is causing so much trouble these days. So that's the offering we're making to the atmosphere. And it's coming into our food supply. One in six women has a level of mercury in her tissues that puts a fetus at risk. We've poisoned our nurturing and supporting matrix.

> The majority of the world's population is struggling with a shortage of the basic necessities for survival, while a small sector of the global economy indulges in a resource feeding frenzy that has destabilized the climate.

Unfortunately, this lack of respect for the natural world and lack of understanding is everywhere in the so-called modern world, and in the striving-to-be-modern world.

During a visit to Delhi, I stayed in a middle-class apartment complex in a very nice area of town. The apartment complex itself was spotless. You could sit down in the middle of the street inside the apartment complex and have your lunch and it was perfectly clean. There was someone hired to go around and wash cars—that was a service provided for residents of the apartment building. But every morning I saw the women on their way to work stopping their cars right inside the guarded gate of the complex to pitch the household garbage over the wall and onto the ground. As soon as you drove out of the apartment complex, you were in a landfill—an uncontrolled landfill in the parlance of environmental regulators. It smelled so bad that you wrapped the end of your scarf around your face when you drove into the place.

In the United States we've managed not to be living in the middle of our own filth on the local level; but on the global level or on the regional level we've created a very high level of interference with all aspects of the ecosystem in terms of the ozone layer, carbon dioxide in the atmosphere, destruction of the ocean ecosystems, and disposal of hazardous and nuclear wastes.

It's time that we looked at our yoga practice in a bigger context. It's time to think about the well-being of the entire world in our actions—and to not only think about it but also in our own hearts to cultivate a sense of the sacred, seeing ourselves and every one of our acts as part of the grand ritual of life. That's what we're missing. And I don't know quite how we get back to that Garden of Eden, that state of paradise. But at least we need to know that it is there, and that the beginning of the journey is to sacrifice greed and to listen to the voice of our heart—to cultivate an inner conscience. And of course there's no better way of doing that than the practice of yoga.

Building Peace Through Diplomacy

Sharon P. Wilkinson

Sharon Wilkinson, the former U.S. ambassador to the Republic of Mozambique and Burkina Faso, is the assistant dean for Global Engagement and diplomat-in-residence at Arizona State University, where she is training the next generation of global leaders in business and diplomacy. Educated at Brown University and the University of Chicago, she speaks English, Portuguese, Spanish, and French, and has served as a professional diplomat in Brazil, Ghana, Portugal, Mexico, the Dutch Antilles, and Washington, D.C.

As a diplomat, I am convinced that there is a role for diplomacy in pursuing the Sacred Link vision, which aims to create a world free of fear, a world in which we honor the sacred ties that unite all human beings. In these pages, I would like to share a few of my experiences in building links that foster harmony and respect across cultural, political, and religious divides.

Everybody knows from reading history or from following current events that any single-minded pursuit of the foreign-policy goals of one's own country to the exclusion of all other considerations leads to isolation and disillusionment. Over the years, I have found that my staff members and I were most successful when we were able to advance our policy goals in ways that projected what is good about America and ourselves while also respecting the policies and goals of our host governments and people—even in situations in which we disagreed. When we stepped

beyond our training and into the respective cultures and
political milieu of our hosts, we were able to understand not
only the foreign-policy goals of their governments but also
the fears, hopes, and aspirations of the citizens. My most
successful staff members did their work with brains *and*
compassion. Working in the local language, they found a
common ground with their contacts at the government,
city, and village level. Let me give you a couple of examples.

In the country of my first assignment, Burkina Faso,
the relations with the government were "correct." That
means we had some serious policy differences, but this
motivated my staff and me to redouble our efforts to connect with the citizens of the country. In Burkina Faso, a
landlocked country that straddles the Sahara, softball is
taken very seriously. My deputy chief of mission, my second in command, was an older Foreign Service officer who
played and coached softball. He used that vehicle to reach
out to the local young men. In the process, he worked with
them on issues of sharing, fair play, and equity. He became
their mentor. My secretary organized a women's softball
team. Together, they brought people from the local community to the softball field.

I firmly believe that those efforts were instrumental in
bringing about a political rapprochement. As I mentioned,
the relations with the government were "correct," which
means not warm and fuzzy. But I invited the president of
Burkina Faso to throw the first pitch of the softball season.
He came. And he pitched. He pitched with perfect cricket
form. And when we had him bat, he batted with perfect
cricket form. It was impeccable. In that moment I realized
that we had gone beyond politics; we had gone beyond our
areas of disagreement and had found a common point of
our own shared humanness.

When I was in Mozambique, I had a staff member

who, on her own initiative, reached out to a group of the young musicians of Mozambique. She recognized their value and wanted to help them build bridges of lifelong connection with other musicians and with their audiences. I was really pleased to hear that three of the young men whom she approached decided to contact another a group of musicians somewhere in the northeast of the country, built a relationship with them, and eventually came to America to share their music with new audiences here.

Here's another example in Mozambique. I had an officer who was a "good old boy" from South Carolina. He had such passion for what he did and such compassion for the Mozambicans. His responsibility was to reach out to the Mozambican business community and to see who was manufacturing what and to help them refine their product, possibly for export to the United States. Now this was a big step in Mozambique. He went all over the country. He spoke to small groups. He spoke to large groups. He spoke in Portuguese. He worked with businesspeople one on one when he found that they had a product that could be exported. With his encouragement and advice, the Mozambicans succeeded in opening up the shrimp-exporting market. He went beyond the requirements of his job, befriending local people and helping them realize their dreams of building successful businesses with international clients.

Also in Mozambique, I had a doctor on my staff who was from Peru. He was responsible for introducing a more systematic approach to the problem of HIV/AIDS. He worked principally with the government, with the Ministry of Health, and other extensions of the Ministry of Health, to institute ways to track the occurrence of the disease and then to introduce programs of prevention, education, and care. Now, in Africa, discussing HIV/AIDS and acknowledging that it is a problem is sometimes a bit tricky. That is not the case in Mozambique, thank goodness. But ministries are ministries. To have somebody from the outside come in and essentially tell you that you're not doing something right is not necessarily welcome. But again, he went about his work with care and compassion; he understood the Mozambicans' hesitancies and their desires, and he figured out how to reach his goal in a way that was not bureaucratic or perfunctory.

Along with these important health and business initiatives, we also bridged the cultural gap in lighter ways. For example, when I was ambassador in Burkina Faso and in Mozambique, we always celebrated the Fourth of July. It was a big deal. We invited our official contacts as well as people who had helped us during the preceding year. We played the U.S. national anthem and the national anthem of the country that we were in—Burkina Faso and later Mozambique. Well, playing a tape recording of the national anthems just wasn't okay with me. It was sterile. It was cold. It was perfunctory. It didn't engage the audience. So I looked for local musicians who would learn our national anthem. On the Fourth of July they performed "The Star-Spangled Banner," and then they performed their own anthem. In Burkina Faso it was really great because I found a gospel choir and put together some of the local musicians. They learned our national anthem and rendered it impeccably. Then with pride they performed their own national anthem.

I read Dolores Woods's article about Swami Vivekananda in *Yoga International* magazine. She writes that it was Swami Vivekananda's view that each nation, like each individual, has a central theme in this life, a principal note around which every other note is arranged to form a harmony. In the United States, the principal note is a mixture of enormous practicality and the belief that nothing is impossible. To quote Swami Vivekananda: "In America is the place, the people, the opportunity for everything. Nothing is rejected because it is new. It is examined on its own merits and it stands and falls by these alone."

I smiled when I read this because it really rang true. When my embassy staff members or my foreign interlocutors would lay problems before me, my mind would grope first for a solution and then, failing that, for an explanation. Impossible was a last-resort word. My approach was to understand the problem, find a way not to make it a problem anymore, and then move on to the next problem. If you look at the countries in which I served—Brazil, Mexico, the Netherlands Antilles, Portugal, Ghana, Burkina Faso, and Mozambique—it's obvious that each of their principal notes would be very different from America's and from mine.

There is one overarching principle that can bring together diplomats and the nations they represent in service to a higher common good. That universal vehicle is non-violence—the habit of not hurting ourselves and not hurting others—taken to the global level.

How can a poor village farmer in Mozambique embrace the notion that she has opportunities and choices as she struggles day to day to provide clean water for her family through droughts and floods? In a remote part of Mexico or an impoverished compound in Ghana, it's not that nothing is impossible, it's that very little seems possible. I couldn't help every disconsolate person I saw in the streets of India or West Africa, nor could I secure jobs for the hordes of unemployed young men in certain cities around the globe. I couldn't promise a bountiful harvest for the villagers we met during our hot and dusty treks around

Africa, and I could not educate every girl who dreamed of having choices in her life. But traveling with eyes wide open, absorbing all the experiences that came our way, my colleagues and I stood in a better position to make policy recommendations that could serve a greater good. To the extent that we were able to play our principal notes in harmony with the people we met, we were able to communicate on a human level.

To be sustainable, peace through diplomacy needs a large context with a more universal vehicle. Up to this point I have suggested that diplomats of the world need to be self-confident, self-aware, modest but strong-willed, empathetic, sympathetic, extroverted, introspective, and endowed with a clear sense of their own strengths and weaknesses and of those of the nations that they represent. If that's not enough, they should be hearty, patient, fearless, good-humored, and ready to depart for any of the four quarters of the world at a moment's notice.

There is one overarching principle that can bring together diplomats and the nations they represent in service to a higher common good. That universal vehicle is nonviolence—the habit of not hurting ourselves and not hurting others—taken to the global level. I like this practical quote from Mahatma Gandhi: "He alone is truly nonviolent who remains nonviolent even though he has the ability to strike. I have had in my life many an opportunity of shooting my opponents and earning the crown of martyrdom. But I had not the heart to shoot any of them, for I did not want them to shoot me however much they disliked my methods. I wanted them to convince me of my error as I was trying to convince them of theirs."

Satyagraha—the power of nonviolence, soul force, the insistence upon truth and nonviolence—is active, strong, and outcome-oriented. If every nation on earth had as its principal foreign-policy objective not to hurt its own interests or the interests of others, then negotiations to bring peace to the Middle East or to stop the ethnic cleansing in Sudan or to stabilize Afghanistan or to set the right course in Iraq would bring a different cast of players to the table. If this were possible, would we still be fighting a war against terrorism?

Pandit Rajmani Tigunait, the spiritual head of the Himalayan Institute, has suggested a systematic approach to embrace nonviolence and to make it an active part of our lives. He identifies nine contemplative steps:

1. Do not kill your conscience.
2. Do not condemn another's way of life.
3. Do not label others.
4. Do not preserve the trash deposited by history.
5. Do not let conventional values overcome love, compassion, and nonviolence.
6. Understand that individuals are an integral part of the same organism.
7. Understand that there is only one life force.
8. Know that hurting others means hurting God.
9. Know that the law of the Divine is the only auspicious law.

Mastering any one of these steps would take a lifetime, perhaps many lifetimes. Nevertheless, they provide an actionable context and a plan for living in a more peaceful world.

I found two of the steps and their accompanying contemplative practices to be especially relevant for my personal and professional growth. The first is Step 2: Do not condemn another's way of life. There are billions of people on this earth living on many continents and in diverse climates, speaking thousands of languages and practicing hundreds of religions or no religion at all. Our differences sometimes seem more important to us than our similarities, and in celebrating the unique natures of ourselves, our families, our communities, our religions, and our nations, we risk devaluing or demeaning others.

Every way of life has its own integrity and reason for being. It is hard to break the habit of judging others by our own standards. As a diplomat, I can't say I never judged others by my standards. It goes with the territory. But over the years and with increased awareness, I did make a conscious effort to monitor my judgmental thoughts and to moderate my conclusions. As Pandit Rajmani says, "Tolerance is the cushion that absorbs the shock of our differences. Tolerance is integral to nonviolence." He suggests a contemplation that is very simple and straightforward.

> Look at the diversity in the world. Certainly it is part of nature. If diversity were not natural, God would have designed all mountains in the same fashion. All humans would have the same faces. People everywhere would have the same skin color. But how boring and redundant that would be. It is the same with lifestyles and values. It is natural for humans to express their diversity in that way, too. Let me not condemn others for how they think or what they think. It doesn't matter whether their values are profound or meaningful to me. Let me learn to respect them and their beliefs exactly the way I want others to respect me and mine.

The next step is Step 4: Do not preserve the trash deposited by history. So many conflicts today arise out of an attempt to right a past wrong, to even the score, to recover what's mine or my ancestors', to prove that you beat me once but you're not going to beat me again, to reclaim the glory of my nation or of my religion. They are rooted in today's memory of yesterday's events.

Memory is key to our sense of who we are. Without the rich fabric of memory, there is no self. Memory is, however, a fragile power that is subject to distortion. What we write and what we pass down through oral history are not actual events but rather the storyteller's interpretation of those events. How much history is written or rewritten according to a political or ideological agenda? And yet these memories inevitably frame our responses to present-day issues. We can't change history, but we can bring a fresh perspective to how we allow its events to inform or influence events of the present that we can control. Here's Pandit Rajmani's contemplation:

> We are all members of the same species. We live on the same planet, consuming the same food and water, breathing the same air, and walking in the light of the same sun. We fight over the same things because we are all human and share the same hunger, thirst, and fear. How sad it is that we remember only war and other disputes and forget the good things we share and the feelings that we have in common. It is a tendency of the human mind to keep careful track of negative, destructive, violent activities and spare barely a moment's thought for the good things. We must reverse this tendency and learn to retain the good memories and let the trash be swept away. Let me find a way

to do this no matter what others do. Let me transform myself and change my habit of remembering the specifics regarding my family, clan, race, especially in relation to people I have formed a habit of disliking and those who I believe dislike me.

By disarming the mind and focusing on our shared characteristics rather than past differences, we move toward tolerance and compassion and away from violence. What if every nation decided to pursue a foreign policy based on the same universal interest—not to hurt itself and not to hurt others? Would that be difficult? Yes. Would it be ridiculous to try? No. Would it be worth the effort? Absolutely. Is it possible? Indubitably. I believe it is a worthy, if vaunted, goal—even if it takes generations to accomplish. Diplomats are perfectly positioned to spearhead this revolution in thought and action. We have the principal responsibility to formulate and carry out our nation's foreign policy. We have extraordinary access to governments and populations. We are trained in the skills of listening, negotiation, advocacy, and persuasion, all of which play a part in the Sacred Link project.

Regardless of profession, we can all begin to take steps today to start the process around the world. Acknowledging our different cultural histories, social mores, and values, we can start to educate our children about tolerance and our shared humanness. In tackling the most intractable challenges to peace today, taking fully into account our different ideologies and systems of governments, national interests, and religious institutions and beliefs, we diplomats can still pull a few more chairs up to the negotiating table. There, among the economic and political experts, the intelligence analysts, and the military strategists, we should also include social anthropologists, psychologists, religious scholars, and global thinkers, thus raising the level of conversation to a point where tolerance and shared humanness become foreign-policy goals.

I close with a quote from Gandhi: "Though mankind is not all the same age, the same height, the same skin, and the same intellect, these inequalities are temporary and superficial. The soul that is hidden beneath this earthly crust is one and the same for all men and women belonging to all climes. There is a real and substantial unity in all the variety that we see around us."

Reclaiming Peace

John Davies, Ph.D.

Co-director of the Partners in Conflict and Partners in Peacebuilding Projects at the University of Maryland, Dr. Davies is an internationally recognized expert in conflict mangement and prevention. He has led conflict transformation initiatives in over twenty countries, including the Middle East, the former Soviet Union, eastern Europe, Asia, Africa, and South America. He has trained hundreds of political leaders, diplomats, negotiators, police, and peacekeepers in peace building and conflict resolution. Serving as a consultant to the U.S. State Department and Department of Defense and the United Nations Department of Peacekeeping Operations, Davies' thoughts on creating peace combine the precision of a professional social scientist with the heart of a deeply concerned human being.

PEACE IS THE NATURAL, DYNAMIC expression of life that is lived in unity. This unity is expressed through acting with integrity, through love, through compassion, through understanding, through people coming together to help each other. We create our own peace through spiritual practice, which opens the inner experience of unity as a present reality. One of the big mistakes of sincere seekers is to regard unity as a goal instead of the immediate reality of the present moment. This is a critical distinction. We need to live from unity now in order to create peace now. By always striving for what is not present, we introduce a separation between ourselves and the present, between ourselves and others' present, and between ourselves and the universe or God or however we choose to think of the highest present reality. Such a separation makes us dependent on external concepts of the world, on the opinion of others, and on accumulating things for our security and even our identity. That dependency leads to fear, which in turn can lead to anger, depression, and further separation from our humanity. Any of those can lead to violence: either inner violence (when we cannot recognize and live our own truth) or outer violence (when people hurt, kill, or undercut the quality of other people's lives).

The core of my work in conflict management is to bring people together and help them experience unity as the basis for peace building. When conflict is across sectarian lines, or across cultures, this also involves coming to appreciate the common truths and experiences that hold across cultures and traditions and bring us together as human beings.

There are four levels of being, four levels of experience, four levels or paradigms for reality that can be called upon to understand and resolve a conflict. By "conflict" I mean whenever our aspirations seem incompatible with someone else's. These four perspectives are reflected in all of the major spiritual traditions, including the Vedic/Hindu, Islamic/Sufi, Christian, Buddhist, Taoist, and Jewish/Kabbalah, as well as in different scientific paradigms. The Vedic *gayatri* mantra, for example, begins with the words *"aum, bhur, bhuva, swaha."* The Sufis speak of the four worlds *(mulk, malakut, jabarut, lahut),* corresponding to the four layers of the heart *(nafs, qalb, ruh, and sirr).* For Christians, the most basic commandment is to "love *God* with all your *heart,* with all your *soul,* and with all your *mind."*

1. The External World of the Object-Oriented Mind

The first level is the external world, the material world of separate objects (bhur or mulk). It is on this external level, where we rely on the outwardly oriented *mind* (nafs), serving the desires of the body and avoiding pain, that we get most easily caught up in separation. We see our problems in the world in terms of the Other. We start to blame others for our pain and become polarized, without looking at our own part in creating it. We get caught up in the duality of good people and bad (or mad) people, dehumanizing the bad. How do we protect ourselves from them? How do we punish and restrain them? In projecting blame, in seeking out the "evildoers," we find ourselves in a war on terrorists and their supporters, with no understanding of why their numbers keep expanding, wasting precious resources with which we could be helping ourselves and others. This is an external understanding of the world.

2. The Internal World of the Heart

The second level marks the entry to the subtle world (bhuva or malakut), the world we experience by opening the higher, more fluid intelligence we call the heart (qalb), rather than just being captive to the lower mind and objects of fear or desire. We move from a place where concrete, separate objects are primary to one where relationships and values are primary and where process and change matter more than structure. This is where we regard our connectedness to other people as more important to us than our own separate, independent existence. Money can buy sex but not love; and shared values of right and wrong hold us together as nations and cultures more strongly than external power, defining our identity more deeply than physical shape and proximity. While we can still be caught up in dualities of good and bad, both internally and with others, the focus is more on the value or principle at stake rather than objectifying people as good or bad, opening the door for rule of law and genuinely inclusive democratic norms and practices.

3. The Realm of the Soul

The third level or perspective on our experience of reality is called the subtlest (swaha, jabarut), the world at the junction point with the divine, corresponding to the essence of our human existence (soul, ruh), the experiencer *(rishi)*. Here, separation from others is really peripheral; we experience ourselves more as a field of awareness than as a separate localized body. We are aware of our essential human nature and the human need that attracts our attention to the qualities and presence of the divine, both within us and in the world around us.

4. Unity, Divinity, Transcendence

This fourth level is experienced as transcending even the separation of the soul from the realm of the divine (aum, lahut). There is no separation, only divine unity, what the Sufis call the *sirr* or secret of our existence. There is no inner and outer, so no exclusion. There is no us and them. There is no good and bad, so no blaming. There is no past and future, only presence. Yet as we become familiar with this world, we experience everything as contained within it—all levels existing as possibilities within the one.

Each of these levels has its own logic; they are different paradigms, all valid methods of understanding and experiencing the world, each with its own value. What we need to understand is how they complement each other, the way each of these levels depends on or is expressed through the other levels.

Based on these four perspectives on our relationship to the world, there are four different approaches we can take to managing conflict and making peace.

On the first, external level, we make sure that we get at least our fair share of the goods that are out there, making sure that we have the strength and the power to avoid dependence. Or, if we don't have that power, we do our best to make sure that we have powerful patrons, people with resources on whose protection we can depend. On this level, politically the emphasis is (unfortunately, in most cases) on hard power, both military and economic. An example is found in the effort to bring peace in Iraq. The assumption was that the United States and its allies could use their superior power to impose democracy from the outside. It is very difficult to impose peace from the outside, and it is extremely rare for a new and sustainable democracy to emerge from such a war.[1]

In moving from blame to understanding the human motivations driving the other side, we also gain a deeper insight into our own needs and possibilities for meeting the needs of both. In helping to rehumanize the enemy, we also rehumanize ourselves.

On the second level, we can manage conflict more effectively by focusing on rights. When we focus on relationships with others, it is not so much who you know that is important, but rather the values that we share as a community. What are the principles or norms of right and wrong that guide us as a community to understand how to treat one another, how to manage conflicts that come up between us? Who goes first through the intersection? What are our rights to speak our ideas, to own property, to intimacy and privacy? What are our children's rights, the rights of women, of minorities? Such rules may be formalized as laws whose legitimacy is based on accord with cultural or national norms and practices, which in turn are rooted in people coming together to find community, family, or organizational consensus as issues arise. People coming together in relationship, to define and affirm what are the norms and values that hold them together, not only creates a meaningful identity for that group but also provides a basis for democratic government and the rule of law, where even the powerful are held accountable and violence can be radically reduced.[2]

For example, the first project I was involved in with the University of Maryland's Center for International Development and Conflict Management was with Edward Azar in the 1980s, when the Lebanon war had been going on for about ten years. The leaders and their negotiators were stuck. Both sides were convinced that the country would split in two—Muslim and Christian. There was little official dialogue and unofficial contacts were too dangerous. In Beirut, a "green line" divided the city and prevented anyone from coming together to talk, through any medium.

To change this dynamic, we found influential, unofficial representatives from both the Muslim and the Christian communities—each of which was internally divided as well. We looked for balance within those communities, and brought people together in Maryland, as there was no way we could do it in Lebanon. We created an environment in which they were able to re-establish relationships long broken by the war. At the end of the first workshop, there was a breakthrough: both sides recognized that the other did not want to break the country in two, that they did indeed want to live together—Muslims and Christians together in one Lebanon.

That realization gave them the momentum for a second workshop in which they started to look for common ground, asking, What is our shared Lebanese national identity? How can we capture that? They set about finding what it was that both sides felt was worth standing for, worth investing their lives for. By the end of the third workshop, they had agreed on a set of twenty principles that represented the reality of Lebanon.[3] They took it back to the political leaders and that then became the basis for negotiating an end to the war, which was completed with the Taif Accords of 1989. The fighting ended and people could begin to re-establish a relatively normal life, though it was only recently that an oppressive Syrian occupation also finally ended in the face of widespread, principled, and nonviolent Lebanese resistance that showed the strength of a peaceful, democratic culture that is holding Christians and Muslims together as one people.

On the third level, peacemaking focuses on the deeper level of our common humanity. Most complex conflicts cannot be settled based only on who is strong or weak, or on who is right or wrong because there are typically many forms of power and many rights and wrongs attributable to various parties, with different norms on what is right in different cultures. Rather, we look for what are the human needs that motivate the parties to fight, in spite of all the risks and loss of life. It might be a need for security, such as for those who fear being imprisoned or killed or losing their livelihood any day. Human security is a need, universally recognizable in any culture, which if denied is inherently stressful. It is also a human need to want respect or recognition for who we are, so that we're not marginalized, suppressed, and alienated. And we need a sense of justice, a sense that we can participate effectively in the larger social, economic, and political environment. There are more, but these are three needs that come up again and again in conflicts, independent of culture.

At this level we can better sustain peace building between cultures and between nations, going beyond cultural consensus to understand each other on a more fundamental level as human beings. In needs-based conflict resolution, the approach is to build trust and a basis of understanding in which each side begins to see the perspectives and motivations of the other. We don't speak about love. Amid such strife, people can't handle the concept of love. The focus is simply on ending the violence and empowering people to meet their needs. That is the language we can use in a violent situation.

But really what we are doing is helping people find a way to love, even under conditions of fear and violence. The first skill on that path is to actively listen to the other side to understand their experience and motivations. What are the human needs underlying their passionate claims of being right? Or of being the righteous victims who are powerless and believe there is nothing they can do because the others are responsible for their suffering. In moving from blame to understanding the human motivations driving the other side, we also gain a deeper insight into our own needs and possibilities for meeting the needs of both. In helping to rehumanize the enemy, we also rehumanize ourselves.

We also coach people in conflict how to deconstruct the images that dehumanize the enemy, and how to speak to each other in ways that don't polarize. How to convey what is true from our direct experience, what values and needs are important to us, without offering assumptions or judgments about the other. This opens the way for building a partnership, building skills that draw on the parties' own cultural resources to creatively address the needs of all parties and transform a conflictive situation toward a sustainable, cooperative relationship. Peace is better understood as an ongoing process, rather than an output or outcome. It requires constant renewal. It's not a matter of imposing peace from the outside but of beginning to live peace through engaging with integrity in a sustainable peace process.

This needs-based, integrative approach to peacemaking is typically done through what is called multitrack diplomacy,[4] working first, as we did in Lebanon, with unofficial ("second-track") opinion leaders who have the flexibility to explore new perspectives. Then the consensus ideas for promoting peace that emerge from this are shared with official ("first-track") decision makers, showing them where they can move toward peace with some confidence they will be supported and their needs addressed. Over the last fifteen years this approach has become widespread and has to be given much of the credit for a remarkable drop in the number and intensity of wars over that time, to less than half the previous level.[5] While there were very few wars settled through negotiation during the Cold War, in the last fifteen years there have been more such settlements than in all the previous two hundred years combined.

> The Sufis say the real war on terror, the real *jihad*, is in facing the fear and violence in our own hearts, not in projecting it out on others.

For example, a few years ago we were asked to help Ecuador and Peru move toward a peace agreement following the third of three wars they had fought over disputed borders. There was a cease-fire, but official negotiations had come to a standstill. We brought together in Maryland unofficial opinion leaders not only from the two capitals but also from the borderland communities where the fighting was taking place and the disputed territory was located. Through this second-track process it became clear the critical need for people on both sides was identity: the land still in dispute was regarded as sacred, important to both nations' sense of identity, not least because of all those who had sacrificed their lives there fighting for their country. Once this was clear, ideas emerged on how to meet the needs of both sides. In one case, the idea was to create a binational park; in another, the land was conceded to Peru but leased back long term to Ecuador with permission for them to honor those who had fought and died there. These ideas were then taken to the two governments, who were persuaded and hired several of the "Grupo Maryland" participants to join the official negotiating teams, and a peace agreement was soon reached including these ideas[6] and sustained through continued engagement of the Grupo Maryland partners in ensuring proper implementation.

The fourth approach to peace is rooted in the experience of unity, the "Sacred Link" that holds us most intimately together. Fear, blame, and anger arise from a sense of profound separation or alienation from others or from God. The experience of unity prevents these from arising: our identity is no longer exclusive, and peace is the immediate reality of our existence. The golden rule—to love others or at least treat them as we would be treated ourselves—which is affirmed in all the great spiritual traditions, is a natural expression of this perspective, no longer just an external norm or constraint. At this level we are the peace—we live it—fulfilling Gandhi's saying that peace is the way, not just the goal.

It doesn't require that the parties' leaders or representatives be experiencing unity. It can be enough that one person is present who is bringing that awareness to the process, or that many in the larger society are experiencing this level: our experience, at this level especially, has an impact on those around us. So in peacemaking, we don't have to talk much about unity or God. Sometimes when we bring together religious leaders from both sides who understand their religions deeply, or when spiritual traditions are strong in the culture, then we can talk about unity and experience the unity together. Short of that, when people are close enough in culture that they can join together in prayers, or spiritual singing (as we did in Lesotho[7]), or even silent prayer or meditation, it can be a profound step toward rehumanizing and reconnecting with one another. However we do it, the goal is to open up the awareness of the parties to a common reality, a common truth—the highest and most sacred truth within us—and look there for guidance on how we can work together and live our lives in harmony.

For example, during the Lebanon war in the mid-1980s, we were able to test the impact on the war of seven successive "peace assemblies" practicing meditation techniques (TM and the TM-Sidhi techniques) together.[8] Over a period of more than two years, seven such groups came together, each large enough and close enough to the fighting for a predicted impact on the war, ranging from fewer than one hundred Muslims and Christians together in the middle of the main area of hostilities at the time, in the mountains outside Beirut, to massive groups of around seven thousand (enough for a predicted global impact[9]) in Europe and the United States. Using independent data sources and analysts unaware of the groups, which lasted from one to eight weeks each, it was found that war deaths dropped by more than 70 percent, from an average of twelve per day to fewer than three per day during the peace assemblies; and cooperation between adversaries increased by more than 50 percent, leading to major breakthroughs in negotiations. These predictions were announced in advance, and all other measurable factors (such as temperature changes, holidays, weekly cycles, etc.) were controlled for, and analyses showed that the impacts began with each assembly (not before) and continued a little beyond them, strongly supporting a causal link. During the three big peace assemblies of seven thousand, terrorist events worldwide—not just those in Lebanon—fell by 70 percent, again as predicted in advance.[10]

It is hard to overemphasize the importance of findings such as these. The most powerful contribution any of us can make toward peace in the world is to live and breathe the reality of peace in our own lives. Our cultural learning pushes us to look outside for answers on conflict and peace building, to those with power, or those able to change the rules, or (at its highest level) those able to help address the needs of those who are suffering and frustrated. We don't pay attention to the enormously rich worlds of the heart, soul, or spirit, and pay the price in a world of violence and terror. The Sufis say the real war on terror, the real *jihad,* is in facing the fear and violence in our own hearts, not in projecting it out on others. It is making peace at this level that most empowers us and allows us to live in a fuller and better world.

Notes

1. M. G. Marshall and T. R. Gurr, *Peace and Conflict 2005: A Global Survey of Armed Conflicts, Self-Determination Movements, and Democracy* (College Park, MD: CIDCM, University of Maryland, 2005). See also www.cidcm.umd.edu.
2. See note 1 above. The risk of war in democratic states is found to be less than half that of autocratic states.
3. E. E. Azar, *The Management of Protracted Social Conflict: Theory and Cases* (Aldershot, U.K.: Dartmouth, Gower, 1990).
4. J. Davies and E. Kaufman, *Second Track/Citizens' Diplomacy: Concepts and Techniques for Conflict Transformation* (Lanham, MD: Rowman and Littlefield, 2002/3).
5. See note 1 above.

6. I. C. Breilh and S. Betancourt, "A Second Way: Grupo Maryland between Peru and Ecuador," in *People Building Peace II: Successful Stories of Civil Society,* ed. P. van Tongeren, M. Brenk, M. Hellema, and J. Verhoeven (Boulder: Lynne Rienner Publishers, 2005).

7. J. Davies, W. Fekade, M. Hoohlo, E. Kaufman, and M. Shale, "Partners in Conflict in Lesotho: Building Capacity for Sustainable Peace," in a forthcoming book edited by the Alliance for International Conflict Prevention and Resolution (Washington, DC).

8. J. Davies and C. N. Alexander, "Alleviating Political Violence: Impact Assessment Analyses of the Lebanon War," *Journal of Social Behavior and Personality* (2005): 285–338.

9. See note 8 above. More than forty published studies now provide consistent evidence of a significant drop in societal violence whenever at least 1 percent is meditating, or when the square root of that number is meditating collectively, using standardized TM and TM-Sidhi procedures. The probability that the results in just this Lebanon study were due to chance is less than one in ten million trillion: one in twenty would have been enough for these findings to be regarded as significant.

10. D. W. Orme-Johnson, M. C. Dillbeck, and C. N. Alexander, "Preventing terrorism and international conflict: Effects of large assemblies of participants in the Transcendental Meditation and TM-Sidhi programs," *Journal of Offender Rehabilitation* 36 (2003): 283–302.

The Elusive Nature of Security

Irene Landers

As a U.S. diplomat working in South America during the 1990s, Irene Landers served as the acting State Department Protocol Officer for the then First Lady Hillary Clinton, coordinating tours for the press and the White House, hosting official diplomatic functions, and organizing volunteer efforts for humanitarian aid for schools, health assessments, and medical assistance in South American villages. Her work afforded her the opportunity to reflect on security and observe the use of fear as a political tool. But her most enduring lessons about security came from interactions with people and situations that challenged her to confront who she really was. Her experiences led her to see that facing fear on a personal level in our daily lives empowers us to see the world in a new light. The mother of two, Landers is also the author of *Exactly Like Me*, an illustrated book that helps children recognize the divine in themselves and everyone they see.

OUR SECURITY—MENTAL, PHYSICAL, and even religious—is constantly breached by others. We think we are secure, but that is just an illusion. When we become aware of this breech, our sense of security is eroded. Fear arises. The greatest menace to our sense of security lies in our own tendency to exaggerate the danger we face, whether it is imagined, perceived, or real. This is true not only for individuals but also for communities and for governments. In this essay, I would like to share some of my experiences as a diplomat in overcoming fear and promoting cross-cultural understanding.

When I lived in Bolivia in the 1990s, I had the luxury of being able to travel to remote towns and villages. I would start my sojourns very slowly. I would just go to a village and have something to eat. I would go back often so that the villagers became accustomed to my face. I would learn their history by talking with them. I realized that many of these villagers had never left their small town. They didn't have cars. They rode bicycles. Many never made it past the fifth grade for girls or eighth grade for boys. They were needed on the farms. They were fishermen and they were farmers.

Everything they knew about politics they were told by their priest, their teacher, or their local politician. A few of them knew how to read. Maybe one would have a television—usually it was the head of the town. So who do you think controlled their sense of security versus fear? Their priest was telling them one thing. The head of the city was telling them one thing. Their teacher was telling them one thing. It was all the same thing. They thought it was the truth.

And how do you think the town leaders got re-elected every year? They would continually raise fears among the villagers. We see it in our own elections. The politicians raise fears, emotionally incite the town, then tell the people how they, the politicians, are going to make the town secure, whether by bringing innovations—roads, electricity, water, commerce, a new soccer field—or by bringing a sense of cultural identity or a newfound sense of sovereignty.

Let's say the people got a new paved road to their village. That would open up the town for commerce. The villagers could begin to sell their homemade items, their agriculture and farming products, and bring in more money. This would enable them to pay for clothing, food, health care and medicine, shelter. Would that make them feel secure? Of course. But consider this. It would bring strangers to their town. Their sense of security becomes elusive again.

I believe that it takes just one person, one stranger, to come into a town and show respect for the villagers—not invade them, not try to change them, just take them as who they are. As a result of that one encounter, they might start to wonder if some of what they have been told is erroneous. That would help dissolve barriers. They could have a new light with which to view their world. They could become less rigid and more open without losing their sense of security. That's within a small village government. Think for a moment of how this same dynamic affects national governments and world leaders. Many times fear has nothing to do with a life-threatening situation. It could arise from a new challenge, an unfamiliar situation in which the stakes are high and people don't know what will happen next.

When I was living as a diplomat in Venezuela in 2000, I found myself in just such a situation. I had been serving as a volunteer manager at the retail store in the embassy. This store purchased homemade items from non-governmental organizations and tribes and sold them to visitors at the embassy. The profits from the sale of those items enabled us to buy more items from the tribes and to donate money to four charitable organizations.

These charitable organizations were a boys' home, a girls' home, a retirement home, and an orphanage for children under the age of six. Every six months I would contact these homes and identify their needs and sometimes assist in making the purchases for them. There were clothes, food, school supplies, books, and computers for the children in the boys' home and the girls' home. The orphanage needed hot-water heaters. They had none. To bathe the babies, the staff had been heating water on the stove. When the children got to be three or four years old, they just took cold showers. The clothes were washed in cold water. So we purchased hot-water heaters for them.

When I asked the nuns who managed the retirement home what they needed, they said nothing. That was great. Three months later I called them back and they still needed nothing. But the third time when I called, the sister said, "We need a mural painted." I was surprised by the serendipity of her request because I am an artist as well as a diplomat, and I've painted murals. So I asked if I could help. She said yes. I went out to meet her, and she took me into a plaza and pointed up to a twenty-by-twenty-five-foot wall on the second story. The size was daunting. I told her I first would need to get permission from the embassy because the retirement home was located in an area that was designated as a dangerous location for Americans. We agreed that I would ask for permission and the sister would try to acquire some scaffolding. The next day the embassy gave me permission and the sister called to say that she had the scaffolding.

So there I was. I wasn't afraid of the area, nor was I afraid of climbing forty feet off the ground on a non-OSHA-approved prop. I had decided to paint a lovely mountain/beach/jungle scene that might remind the residents of their youth. I had the design in my head. I went back to the retirement home the next day to finalize the details and purchase the paint. Out of courtesy I decided to ask the sister what she wanted painted. I was a bit shocked by her reply, to say the least. She asked if I would please paint the Virgin de Lourdes on the wall. I'm not Roman Catholic. I didn't know who the Virgin de Lourdes was. I had somebody with me who said it was the Virgin Mary. In France she did a lot of healing. She's in a cave by a river. Oh my. I was being asked to paint a fifteen-foot depiction of the Virgin Mary in a cave in France on a wall and have it done in less than one month. This was going to take some doing.

The whole experience really made me think about fear and security. Up until that moment, fear had not restricted me in any way from enlarging my sphere of friends and acquaintances in this foreign country. Fear for my own safety did not stop me from volunteering in a dangerous neighborhood or from painting. But when I was told the subject matter, it took my breath away. Nevertheless, I made the choice to be courageous. I went to the mental edge. The next day I purchased the paints and supplies. I looked for pictures of the Virgin de Lourdes on the Web. All I found was a beautiful woman in a blue dress with gold trim. Nothing that I could really work with. Hmm, I thought, it's going to be a bit of a challenge to paint her.

> It's finding that sacred spot within yourself that completes the process of becoming an effective peacemaker because you will no longer be run by fear.

The next day I did a short meditation, then I started to climb the rickety scaffolding. Up, up I went, taking the board from below and putting it on the scaffolding above. The nuns could get only two boards six feet long by twelve inches wide. But I had promised. I got to the top and thought: This is where I will start the mural because I'm not going to climb back down and think about this again. I taped a string to the top and let the ball fall to the ground. That was how I was going to paint her straight.

The residents of the retirement home kept walking by the scaffolding, looking at me and making the sign of the cross. I would look down to them and say, "Thank you, please pray for me." It was about 10 a.m., and I didn't know that mass was going to begin.

I tied a rope to the top of the scaffolding where I was. I had to climb back down again, tie all my paint cans to the rope, climb back up the scaffolding, and hoist all the paint up to the top.

But that wasn't the worst of it. I hadn't even done a drawing. I had agreed to paint the mural only the day before. No preliminaries, nothing. I let go. I meditated. I surrendered. And then I began to draw in chalk. Just the head. A fifteen-foot person drawn by someone standing on scaffolding with two boards, one to hold my paints and one to support my weight. That was all I had. It's not as if I could go up and down drawing this person. I had to start from somewhere so I started from the head. It took about three hours.

I was so proud of myself. I had the Virgin looking up to heaven. Wonderful. I climbed down and the residents were just as pleased as they could be—chattering, laughing, smiling. The sister came up to me and said, "Oh, this is wonderful but could you have the Virgin looking down to the plaza?"

I can laugh about this now. I can laugh because I surrendered not to my fear but to my courage. I said, "Sure, I'll go back up there and paint her again tomorrow." The next time I came back I painted the head with the gaze looking down to the plaza. And every day for the next few weeks I went and painted with no drawing and surrendered to my courage. I surrendered to my sacred spot and found the bond.

In facing unknown fears, we have the opportunity to find our center, our balance, and courage. Then we can move past it all. I was challenged. I got the opportunity to see the smiling faces every day when I climbed down from the scaffolding. Every morning at 10 a.m. I listened to the choir of mass, the chants. And I'm sure they were praying for me. The sister came up to me afterward and told me she always knew I could do it. Was I paid for the mural? Oh, a thousand times over in their smiles, their prayers, their pats on the back. Just to see them at the bottom of the plaza spending their days meditating on this figure was more than I could ever have asked for.

In Bolivia, I faced fear of a different kind. Because of our status as diplomats, my family and I lived in a mansion—a six-thousand-square-foot house. The yard was surrounded by a wall twelve feet high and one foot deep. On top of the wall was cemented glass. On top of the glass was barbed wire. That was just to get into the yard. The house itself was wired with an alarm. We even had a safe room because, in 212 years of independence, Bolivia has had 240 coups. We had our own generator and our own huge water supply. We were quite secure—or so we thought.

My husband's mission took him away from home a lot, but I still felt safe in this foreign country until one night when my son walked in at about two in the morning and said he heard noises downstairs. Now, downstairs was large. We had two kitchens, two dining rooms, and a couple bathrooms. I got up, turned on all the lights upstairs. The first thing I saw as I walked downstairs was the green light to the alarm. That meant the alarm was armed. But the door from the garage to the house was open. I shut it, locked it, and went all over the house, checking every room. Nothing was disheveled. None of the cabinets were opened, none of the silver or china disturbed. I thought that maybe the wind had blown open the garage door and that was what my son had heard. I didn't connect the fact that the alarm light was green yet the door was open. I just shut it and locked it.

I went back to bed and about an hour and a half later my son woke me up again and said he heard more noises in the house. So I got up again, and went through the same routine. When I went downstairs and saw that the garage door was open again, I knew that somebody had been in the house. I called the regional security officers in the embassy and they came out. It was about four in the morning. They didn't find anything, but they posted somebody outside the wall until they could do a search the next morning. When they did, they found that part of the alarm system didn't work: the battery to the garage door had been dead for three years.

It turned out that the robbers had climbed up the lamppost outside our patio, jumped onto the patio roof, and entered the house through the back, where the employees were living. From there they went into the garage and then into the house, looking for a way to open the garage so that they could steal the car. The embassy posted somebody at our house for the next few nights. Because it was late, the guard naturally fell asleep. The robbers came back, using the same route, and somehow got into the car. This time the alarm went off. Well, everybody heard that and the robbery was averted.

Was I afraid during all of this? Well, naturally, in the beginning I wasn't afraid because I thought I was secure. But the first night I had locked the robbers into the house. They were probably more afraid than I was. Here they were, locked in a house unfamiliar to them, in the dark, at risk of being arrested. When I reawakened later in the night and discovered that there had been a break-in, I was afraid, at least temporarily. But I soon regained my sense of security.

In becoming a diplomat I had received all kinds of training to protect myself and others. All this training made me confident that I could handle any situation. This did not mean that my security was not breached. It was. But I felt secure in knowing that I could call upon my training to bring me back to balance and know what to do. And because I had invested so much time in understanding Bolivian culture, I knew that it was not a violent society. They were poor people, some of whom would steal what they could and sell it on the black market. If they had wanted to kidnap me, they would have done it.

Also in Bolivia, I volunteered at an orphanage that had newborns, toddlers, and children up to seven years old. There were so few paid workers in this orphanage that the babies went untouched during the day. It was not because the workers were unwilling or because they knowingly neglected the babies but because there wasn't enough time or hands. The babies' backs became rigid from not being touched except when they were fed three times a day. When we fed them, we sat them up between our legs so that two babies could be fed at the same time. When you picked them up, they went straight as a board and cried. It took lots of touching and nurturing and cuddling to get those babies to release.

We are the same way. Be willing to stretch beyond your barriers and not become rigid. Rigidity becomes the barrier, the limitation, and then you live in fear. Know you have barriers and have compassion for them as well as respect for others, who also have them.

You will understand when you are faced with someone who is reflecting fear to you. You can see it in their eyes, in their face, in their body language. You can see it in their actions and their words. See yourself reflected in them no matter whom you are with. You may not understand the depth of their fear, but by being secure within yourself, you will radiate that sense of security, freedom from fear, and peace. It's finding that sacred spot within yourself that completes the process of becoming an effective peacemaker because you will no longer be run by fear. No matter what uniform we wear, no matter what mask we put on, we must find that sacred spot within ourselves. Only then can we become part of the Sacred Link and create a sacred bond with others.

From Prison to Ashram

Kiran Bedi, Ph.D.

Kiran Bedi has lived her life defying expectations and encouraging others to follow her dynamic example. By age twenty-three she was an all-Asia tennis champ and had become the first woman ever to join the Indian Police Service. During her long and distinguished career, she has stood her ground against angry protestors, introduced preventative policing, and once had the prime minister's car towed for a parking violation.

She gained international recognition as a force for social change in the early 1990s, when she undertook the reform of India's most notorious prison. "I delivered to the prisoners the spirit of my family, my values, and the whole experience of my learning," she says. That spirit includes respect for open communication and a commitment to self-transformation through education.

Bedi holds a Ph.D. in Drug Abuse and Domestic Violence and in 1994 received the Ramon Magsaysay Award (Asia's Nobel Peace Prize) for her efforts to humanize the Indian prison system.

I HAVE WORKED IN THE INDIAN POLICE SERVICE since 1972, when I became the first woman officer in India. I spent most of my life policing the city of Delhi, until I was sent to Mizoram, in northeast India, on the border of Myanmar and Bangladesh. In our professional terms, it was what's called a hard-area posting, meaning that I had to move very far from my family. The rule is that, after being posted in northeast India, a police officer returns to mainstream policing. It was assumed that I would return to lead the Delhi police force, which is considered a high-profile assignment. There are about sixty thousand police officers there, with all the necessary infrastructure and facilities. Everybody salutes you because you are in a position of power, not necessarily because you deserve it.

But when I returned from Mizoram, nobody was willing to secure a post for me in the Delhi police force. I waited and waited on a compulsory wait, a paid holiday. I treasured this time because such sabbaticals do not often fall in one's lap. Perhaps the failure to give me an assignment was intended to put me, an independent-minded woman who had broken the gender barrier to join the Indian Police Service, in my place. But I thought, "These people are fools. They don't understand what they've given me. They may be waiting, but I'm not." So I walked, I relaxed, and I started to write. I could have appealed to the powers that be—the minister of home affairs and the prime minister—for my next assignment in Delhi. But I didn't. I let them be so that they'd let me be. During those nine months I wrote the first eight chapters of my biography, *I Dare*. By then, the government accountants finally woke up: *somebody's collecting a salary to write?* They suddenly decided that I needed to be posted somewhere. In the Indian Police Service, one can be transferred from police work to prison work and back again—it's a British legacy. And so I was sent to head Tihar, a two-hundred-acre complex comprised of four prisons in New Delhi. With ninety-seven hundred prisoners, it is one of the largest such institutions in the world.

The news of my assignment came out in the papers—as God would have it, everything I do, right or wrong, comes out in the papers in India. The headlines read KIRAN BEDI IN PRISON. People said Kiran Bedi was sent to the right place, where she belonged. My colleagues wanted to see me out of the way because I defined policing as the power to make a difference, the power to serve. Some of my colleagues, who thought they were competing with me for seniority and high positions, hated me for this definition. Through that service, a lot of innovative policing had come about over the years, and inevitable comparisons were made in the media: If Kiran can do this, why can't you? If Kiran can handle drug-abuse problems and other issues, why can't her male colleagues? Somebody in the press quipped, "Kiran is the only man in the Delhi police." No wonder my colleagues wanted me in prison. Ironically, that job at Tihar led to a dream assignment at the United Nations. But at the time, it was seen as a slap in the face.

I met with my predecessor at Tihar and asked him, "How is it?" He said, "Kiran, don't go there." When I asked why, he said, "There's no work for you there. There were just two files there, and I didn't even go to the prison to work. I used to get the two files sent to my home. I'd go in once in a while to show my face, and that's it." Obviously, he knew that I don't like to sit around doing nothing. I like to work. But I didn't share my thoughts with him. I just said, "Thank you very much."

I began my work at Tihar by asking myself, What am I here for? The answer, I decided, was as follows: I'm here to see that the prisoners' time is utilized in a worthwhile manner, in a manner that they realize has been worthwhile. It's not about killing time but rather investing for the future. And that's what I used to tell these prisoners, thousands of them.

When I came to Tihar, there were ninety-seven hundred prisoners—men, women, and children. (In the Indian prison system, a woman can keep her child with her in prison if it's for the child's security. And today there are hundreds of children in prison, but that's another story in itself.) On my first day of work at the prison, I wore a dress with full sleeves and I wore tennis shoes. I wanted to send a message with my tennis shoes: I've come here to walk, not just to talk my work but to walk my work. When I arrived at the prison entrance, there were a lot of prisoners waiting to be taken to court. I stepped in and was greeted by a huge number of amazed glances. This was the first time in history that a woman had been chosen to head a prison of this size anywhere in the world. Therefore, the men were wondering, How is it going to be? Is she going to come in uniform surrounded by guards and say, "Left, right, left"? Or is she going to walk around? Is she going to listen? Is she going to be scared? There were lots of questions even though many prisoners already knew me because, as a police officer, I had sent them to prison in the first place.

As I approached the prisoners at the entrance, they looked at me and I looked at them. I didn't look down, as a woman might when faced with the stares of so many men. For a few seconds we looked at each other. I walked closer to them, wondering, Where do I begin? What do I say? What do I want to do here? In their faces I saw deprivation. I saw sadness. I saw isolation. I saw grief.

From those thoughts I broke the ice by saying, "Do you pray?" They all looked at me and no one answered. I said again, "Do you pray?" Still, they didn't answer. There were a few prison guards with me and when I walked closer to the prisoners, they used their sticks to drive them back for fear one of the prisoners would pounce on me. My predecessor, the former inspector general at Tihar, had his finger bitten off by a prisoner. Thereafter, the prisoners were kept behind a grille whenever the inspector general made his rounds.

Once again I asked, "Do you pray?" They didn't answer, probably because they were too scared of the guards to speak. So I told the guards to lower their sticks. One last time, I asked, "Do you pray?" Someone replied, "Sometimes." "What kind of prayer?" I asked. Some said they read scriptures. Others said they recited a mantra. "Good, excellent. Would you like to pray now?" They said yes. We all shut our eyes and recited a prayer, which essentially says we are all your people, God. Make us do all that is right and think all that is right. I don't know if the guards sang or not, but the prisoners and I sang. And after the prayer was over, some composure and peace had returned to the courtyard. I found smiles on the men's faces. And my fingers were still intact. That was the power of prayer. When I saw the transformation, I just walked away. I had nothing more to say for the moment. That was the beginning of an amazing journey that has continued to this day, a journey I believe will continue for the rest of my life.

What are the lessons I took from the experience at Tihar? First, have respect for whatever you receive. Second, be grateful for whatever you receive. Third, be at peace with whatever you receive. Fourth, put your heart and soul into whatever you receive. Fifth, add joy and life to whatever you receive. And finally, leave the results to destiny. That's what happened in my life at this prison and in all my career assignments before and after.

This is what I did at Tihar. As soon as I walked in, I sensed it was a place of isolation, a dumping ground, an institution organized around the idea of punishment. I have always believed in corrective policing. For me, policing has never been punitive. It's not about sending people to prison. It's about showing them the route to correction, and that may come through prison. When I asked the prisoners if they prayed, I was essentially asking them if they were seeking forgiveness and help. At Tihar, I had the opportunity to put my beliefs in action, to prove what I had been saying all along. For me, policing was a cause, not a career. After that first day, the prayer was followed by yoga. Soon there was satsang, lessons, spiritual music, song, and dance. The prisoners told their visitors about the changes, and word quickly spread through the community. Brahma Kumari, a spiritual organization, was right across the street. Its members came and asked to do satsang inside the prison. "Will you allow us?" they asked. I said, "Right now!" The prisoners came, and the Brahma Kumari women in white started to spread the message of nonviolence, peace, and harmony. Soon the newspapers were reporting that the winds of change were blowing inside the prison walls.

During my first weeks at the prison, as yoga and meditation became part of the prisoners' routine, I was also busy reviewing the prison manuals and memorizing the rules and regulations. One lesson that I've learned in my career is that when you begin a new assignment, the first month is vital. By the fourth week, your colleagues know who you are. When I held my first meeting with my colleagues, I asked them, "Do you know why we are here at Tihar? One of them said, "To ensure that nobody runs away from here." "Full marks," I said. "Obviously, if anybody runs away, you and I are in trouble." They assured me that there was an excellent record at Tihar—nobody had managed to run away. "Excellent. Wonderful," I said. "Please keep it like that."

Then someone else said, "We are here to make sure that riots don't happen inside the prison." When I asked how they maintained order, my colleague said, "If we detect any unrest, we immediately punish the perpetrator and put him in an isolation cell so that he learns the lesson of his life." I said, "We'll ensure that there are no riots at Tihar," but I didn't say how.

Next, a colleague said, "The prisoners ask for lots of permissions—they want newspapers, wristwatches, pens, and books. Part of our job is to reject their requests." I said, "Excellent. You reject them. But let's look again at the rule." I asked them to open their prison manuals to such-and-such a page. They didn't have their manuals. I asked them to get their manuals and together we reread the passage. It said that the following items were not permitted: books, wristwatches, transistor radios, televisions, and so on. And the last words came after a comma: "*unless permitted.*" I said, "Now let's draw a line under the words *unless permitted.*"

Even though the rule said they could permit these items, my colleagues explained that they always rejected the requests. "We let the prisoners go to court and then the court decides. It's an expensive procedure, and it takes time to get to court, and by then the prisoners realize the power of law." When I asked what typically happened in court, they explained that sometimes the court overruled them and sometimes it upheld their decisions. The process, they admitted, was time-consuming and embarrassing. "Sometimes we sit in the dock and the criminal also sits in the dock and we're like two equals." We agreed that it would be best if this whole proceeding could be avoided.

> All I did from my childhood until now—and I pray that God gives me the wisdom to continue—is to ask myself: Is my today better than yesterday? Did I do all the right things yesterday and what can I do better tomorrow? Am I continuing to grow?

"Now, my friends," I said, "this is my first instruction as head of the prison. Books, wristwatches, and pens are permitted, unless rejected." My first written instruction was posted on all notice boards in the prison. That was the beginning of an amazing transformation. I didn't walk in thinking that that one decision would change so much or that it would leave a legacy of a whole new model for prison management. Instead, I began my work at Tihar by asking myself, What am I here for? The answer, I decided, was as follows: I'm here to see that the prisoners' time is utilized in a worthwhile manner, in a manner that they realize has been worthwhile. It's not about killing time but rather investing for the future. And that's what I used to tell these prisoners, thousands of them.

We had an evening meeting every day. I would say, "Listen, you and I are not different in any way. The only difference is that you spent your time one way and I spent my time in another way." I asked them if they wanted to adopt some of my ways. They said yes. "Then I'll tell you what I did. And there's nothing mysterious about it. All I did from my childhood until now—and I pray that God gives me the wisdom to continue—is to ask myself: Is my today better than yesterday? Did I do all the right things yesterday and what can I do better tomorrow? Am I continuing to grow?

And where does this wisdom come from? It comes from learning, it comes from books, it comes from teachers, it comes from self-awareness, it comes from environment. One has to be selective. I told them, "You can watch a pornographic film or you can watch a remarkable documentary that changes your life. You can go to a place that poisons you or to a place that purifies you. The same legs will carry you to a place of destruction or to a temple." I reminded them, "You and I have been using the same legs. Maybe the directions were different. Similarly the hands. You were using them to pick pockets. Maybe I was using the hands to write and to serve others. The hands are the same, the legs are the same, the head is the same. It's the utility that's different." I kept sharing this with them. I invited spiritual speakers to come to say the same thing.

Under my leadership, the entire prison became a place of education. All ninety-seven hundred prisoners received two hours of education each morning, as well as spirituality hour in the evening, games in between, and plenty of books. You might wonder where the books and teachers came from. Because there was no money, I asked for donations of used schoolbooks, and they came by the truckload from the outside community. As soon as a prisoner entered the prison, he was asked to fill out a form. It didn't say, "What crime?" because that was already written on his page. Instead the form asked, "What educational level?" Prisoners were given a schoolbag and books and were told to report to their classroom the following day.

The teachers were the prisoners themselves. We identified the ones who had something to teach. "You're a lawyer? A twelfth-grade graduate? You know French? You know the Tamil language? You can teach English? Come on." We made a databank of educated prisoners who could teach and put them through a teacher-training program. We never talked of crime or the reasons they had been sent to Tihar. Suddenly the prisoners realized they were getting a new identity.

Another thing I did was to separate gang members from the mainstream prison population. I initiated a separation between high-security prisoners and those in medium security. This meant the gang members could not recruit other prisoners. That was one of the most vital and most challenging endeavors of my career. The prisoners challenged me in court, but the judge stood by me, perhaps because the media had already created an image of Tihar as a place of reform. The community was already with me for having opened up the system. By the way, there were three hundred foreigners inside the prison, and they were writing letters to *The Times* of London, *The New York Times, The Washington Post,* and *The Guardian,* saying that there were major changes underway at Tihar. So the embassies came out in my favor. There was a new pressure on my government, and the officials started to say, "My God, where the hell have we sent this woman?"

Another innovation was the creation of a feedback box so that the prisoners could tell me what was going on in the prison. Interestingly, this feedback box was a mobile box that traveled from barrack to barrack. Only I had the key to the box. From it I received tips about inmates who were abusing drugs, guards who were accepting bribes, and other infractions. The prison staff could never claim that the inspector general needed to be briefed on internal prison matters. On the contrary, I briefed them.

Remember the tennis shoes I wore on my first day? I walked the prison every day. That's being on the ground floor. Essentially, what I delivered to the prisoners was the spirit of my family, my values, the whole experience of my learning. I came to see a sacred link between the prisoners and me. I've always believed that if I'm in a position of power, my duty is to give. Instead of depriving and dehumanizing the prisoners, I wanted to serve them.

Education and an opportunity to pursue a spiritual path—that was my legacy. A time came when the prison was at peace. There were no riots. There were no escapes. There was no violence and the prisoners could read, they could write, they could listen to what was going on in the world.

The crowning glory of the reforms at Tihar was the meditation program. When I was trying to think of how to change the prisoners' mind-sets, one of my officers suggested Vipassana meditation, an ancient practice used by the Buddha twenty-five hundred years ago. My colleague explained that Vipassana centered on self-transformation through self-awareness. Intrigued, I rang up Guru Goenkaji and said, "Can you help me?" He agreed, on the condition that I allow him and the other teachers to stay inside the prison during this program. I consented and before long the first ten-day course began.

The teachers stayed inside the prison, and for the first six days, they were threatened by the prisoners, who told them to leave. But by the seventh day, the prisoners wanted them to stay. On the eleventh day, when they broke silence, I found many of the prisoners crying before the CNN and the BBC cameras that were inside the prison to document the experience. "Didn't you know you were before a camera?" I asked one prisoner. He responded, "I am free within, Madam. I am free. I am in the prison by law but I am free within. I am now free to say that I was a criminal. I was revengeful. I did the murder. I was going to kill the person who had delivered this judgment against me, but now I seek forgiveness. I will tell the court, 'Free me or punish me as much as you want, but at some stage I will also walk free because I am free within.' I have said what I wanted to say. The burden is off my chest." The Vipassana meditation experiment was chronicled in a film called *Doing Time, Doing Vipassana*. My book *It's Always Possible* charts the larger transformation of Tihar from a place of criminality to one of humanity.

> I told the prisoners, "You can watch a pornographic film or you can watch a remarkable documentary that changes your life. You can go to a place that poisons you or to a place that purifies you. The same legs will carry you to a place of destruction or to a temple."

Out of my experiences at Tihar came a new model for prison management. I called it the Three Cs Model: Collective, Corrective, and Community-based. It was collective because prisoners became participants through the feedback box, through education, through collective supervision, and through spiritual, artistic, and vocational training. It was corrective in objective and it was community-based because, ultimately, it was the community that would receive these people back in their midst. The success of the Three Cs Model at Tihar has inspired reforms in prisons not only in India but also around the world.

Seeds of Hope

Ishan Tigunait

Growing up at the Himalayan Institute, Ishan Tigunait received his first lesson in personal development and progressive leadership from the illustrious master of the twenty-first century, Swami Rama of the Himalayas. After receiving his B.S. in computer engineering, he joined the corporate world, working for IBM. But he soon moved on to fulfill his ambition of establishing a business model where corporate profitability is guided by a higher vision of self-empowerment and social regeneration. He is a founding director of Human Energy and a board member of Roshini Biotech, market leaders in large-scale biofuel plantations based on sustainable community models in Africa and India, respectively. He is also director of the Himalayan Institute's Global Humanitarian Initiative.

One of Sacred Link's most exciting humanitarian projects, the Biofuel Rural Development Initiative was launched in drought-stricken South India in 2003. The project promotes reforestation, soil conservation, and a return to the natural balance of rural life.

FOR COUNTLESS GENERATIONS, rural India ran on the *jajmani* system in which every family in a village was considered a "client" of all the others. Almost everything the community needed could be produced within the village, and essential goods and services were exchanged without the use of currency. The washermen, for example, collected and laundered the clothes of the entire village, and in return collected pots from the potters, rope from the rope makers, and vegetables and grain from the farmers; the barbers cut their hair, and the tailors made their clothes.

This natural interdependence ensured that the basic necessities were available to everyone and that nothing was wasted. The owner of a field harvested only what he needed, and when he declared himself finished with his harvest, the other villagers could come and take what remained. When the harvest was complete, villagers could turn their livestock out to graze in the fields. The same attitude applied to fruit trees. It was understood that only the landowner was entitled to pick the fruit, but anyone—even a passing stranger—was entitled to fruit that had fallen.

The jajmani system created a stable economy, for everyone understood that if any segment of the community struggled, everyone would suffer. As a result, social and economic interrelationships were carefully nurtured to maintain the health of the village and the land that supported it. And because farmers provided the nourishment needed to sustain life, they occupied a central role in this time-honored system.

Today this traditional way of life has all but vanished. The causes are many and complex: changes in India's political structure, the redistribution of land, the introduction of modern conveniences, and the switch to a cash economy, to name only a few. In addition, the introduction of modern farming methods during the Green Revolution of the 1970s made the villagers dependent on outside markets for chemical fertilizers, heavy machinery, fuel, and in some cases even seeds. No longer self-sufficient, villagers must now purchase the supplies they need to grow their crops. The costs of production have increased, while the selling price of agricultural products has remained stagnant. In the South Indian state of Andhra Pradesh, 70 percent of the state's seventy-eight million residents work the land to make a living, but instead of being the vital center of a vibrant economy, farmers can now barely survive.

To make matters worse, severe drought plagues South India. The monsoon rains, which normally supply most of the irrigation water, have become increasingly unreliable. In the absence of rains, the only way to get water is to drill deep tube wells to tap underground aquifers. But drilling a well is prohibitively expensive for the average farmer, as is the long-term cost of operating one. Because the electricity required to pump the water to the surface is produced by small diesel generators, expensive fuel, which the farmers cannot afford, must also flow into the village.

The economic drain created by modern farming methods, coupled with the chronic water shortage, has meant that most farmers can barely afford to grow crops. They can afford failed crops even less. Yet as the entire region bakes in the sun, crops are failing by the fieldful. There is no money for necessities and little food for their families. Farmers mortgage everything they own to see them through the next harvest, and often fall victim to high-interest moneylenders. Saddled with interest rates as high as 50 percent, they spiral further and further into debt.

For many, the misery of the seemingly endless cycle of poverty gripping their families became unbearable. Tired of struggling to make ends meet through year after year of persistent drought, crushed by insurmountable debt, and humiliated by their inability to support their families and fulfill their other social obligations, many men committed suicide. From 1996 to 2004, thousands of farmers in Andhra Pradesh ended their own lives.

The suicide epidemic is only the most obvious symptom of the social upheaval throughout the rural agricultural communities of South India. The complex web of relationships, which once served as a safety net for all the villagers, vanished with the passing of the jajmani system. The goods and services that once created strong community ties and a healthy sense of interdependence are now merely commodities to be bought and sold. A way of life has vanished; and with nothing sustaining to replace it, the fabric of rural society has begun to unravel.

As the plight of the villagers worsened throughout the 1990s, scientists from various disciplines began to look for new ways to foster sustainable rural development. A group at the Indian Institute of Sciences in Bangalore had been researching these strategies for more than thirty years. In the late 1990s they were searching for ways to bring electricity to run irrigation pumps to remote, drought-stricken areas. One day, as they were discussing the possibilities with some villagers, their eyes fell on the large trees that formed hedges and boundary markers around the parched fields. Despite the persistent drought, the trees were flourishing.

These were pongamia trees. Mature specimens of *Pongamia pinnata* stand up to fifty feet high, and their dense canopy can be almost equally wide. They sport hearty, dark green leaves that retain moisture even under intense heat. Small clusters of white, purple, and pink flowers blossom on their branches throughout the year, maturing into brown seedpods that litter the ground. The pods are so tough that even goats ignore them. Other than firewood, the only known use for the pongamia trees was to provide shade.

But as much as they appreciated the shade, it was the seeds that held the researchers' attention. They knew that before the introduction of kerosene lanterns, pongamia seeds had been a source of lamp oil. This gave them an idea. Back in their laboratory, they found that, with minimal refinement, pongamia oil could also be used to fuel diesel engines.

This discovery addressed one of the most pressing needs of rural villages—the ever-growing demand for energy. Instead of importing petroleum diesel fuel to run their irrigation pumps and to power the generators that are the main source of electricity in remote areas, the villagers could switch to a locally available, affordable fuel. With further processing, pongamia seed oil can also be used to run heavy machinery and tractors—even to fuel cars and trucks.

Since the late 1990s, members of the Himalayan Institute's South India Chapter had been concerned by the calamity facing the villagers. Under the leadership of Anil Reddy, the Institute had been working to provide basic medical and counseling services, as well as some small-scale employment opportunities in the form of organic farming projects in some villages. As helpful as these efforts were, it was clear that they were only short-term solutions. What the villagers really needed was a sustainable way to earn their living and a means of renewing their self-confidence and their traditional community bonds.

> The economic drain created by modern farming methods, coupled with the chronic water shortage, has meant that most farmers in South India can barely afford to grow crops.

Searching for a way to bring this about, Reddy and his colleagues investigated dozens of rural development strategies. Pongamia was the most promising. For one thing, the tree is well suited to the intense heat and sunlight of South India. For another, its dense network of lateral roots and its thick, long taproot make it drought resistant. The tree can even help rehabilitate the land—the dense shade it provides slows the evaporation of surface water and its root structures promote nitrogen fixation, which moves nutrients from the air into the soil. And once established, the pongamia can give a reliable harvest of seeds for fifty years.

After meeting with the researchers from the Indian Institute of Sciences and conducting additional research, Reddy knew he had found what he was looking for—a way to restore the self-reliance and economic self-sufficiency that had once been the hallmark of village life. Pongamia could form the basis of a self-sustaining agricultural platform that would breathe new life into the villages. Using pongamia oil to run irrigation pumps and generators would stem some of the outflow of village resources, but that was only the beginning. In addition to biofuel, pongamia provides other resources vital to a farming community. The seedcake remaining after pressing the oil can be used as cattle feed; crops can be treated with organic pesticides made from the seedpod; kitchen stoves can run on methane biogas made by fermenting the seedcake; and the waste pulp from the fermented seedcake can be used as an organic fertilizer. The potential was tremendous. And best of all, planting and cultivating the tree would require the labor of many villagers. Not only would this provide a steady income, but they would have to learn to rely on each other and share resources if the enterprise was to blossom. With millions of acres of farmland lying barren and unused, this tree could breathe new life into the villages of Andhra Pradesh.

After experimenting with a small pilot project to test the feasibility of the idea and to iron out the glitches, the Himalayan Institute launched its Biofuel Rural Development Initiative in 2003 in collaboration with two other organizations: Rahul Medical Society and Roshini Biotech. The ultimate goal of this project is to develop the full potential of the pongamia tree to bring about a widespread and lasting renewal throughout the region's rural villages. But for this to happen, Reddy and his colleagues knew that they would first need to rekindle the villagers' capacity for hope. For this project to succeed on a grand scale, the impetus would have to come from the farmers themselves.

The Institute began by launching a massive public awareness and education campaign. It sent teams from village to village. They erected tents and provided cool lemon drinks and other refreshments; they listened to the villagers talk about their failing crops, the problems caused by the high-interest money-lenders, and their anxieties about the future. Then, team members offered a solution: grow pongamia trees as a crop. It was a radical idea—cultivating a common shade tree as a cash crop. But the team members assured the farmers that they had buyers for all the tough, brown seedpods these trees could produce.

The villagers were amazed to hear that they could grow pongamia on land they had considered useless. Rocky, hilly parcels were perfectly suitable for the tree. This allayed the farmers' fears of gambling on an unknown crop—they realized they could cultivate pongamia on their marginal land while continuing to grow traditional crops on their most fertile acreage. And they were surprised to hear that the water required for four acres of crops such as rice or millet could support up to 150 acres of pongamia. Villagers also learned about crops that grow especially well

> A way of life has vanished; and with nothing sustaining to replace it, the fabric of rural society has begun to unravel. Years of mistrust and hard times had strained the traditional bonds of fellowship that hold rural communities together. Now it was time to renew them.

in the vicinity of pongamia. For example, one of the more unusual characteristics of the tree is its capacity to attract and withstand insects that weaken and kill other plants. These pests restrict themselves to the pongamia and ignore more delicate plants, such as the cotton or groundnut. With the cooperation of the village councils, the word began to spread, and soon thousands were flocking to local meetings to learn about this promising new project.

The idea began to take hold, and when a significant number of farmers were ready to try it, the Institute set up workshops to teach the fundamental skills: how to irrigate and care for the seedlings during the crucial first few years, how to prune the growing trees, and how to graft the plants. Grafting is necessary because it can take as long as ten years for a tree in the wild to reach full seed-bearing maturity. Even when it finally matures, there is no guarantee the tree will consistently produce a good harvest. If they were to grow pongamia successfully, the villagers needed simple, effective, and inexpensive ways to overcome these limitations.

In Roshini Biotech's Hyderabad laboratory and on expansive test plots, researchers had developed standardized techniques for growing pongamia on a large scale. They found that to guarantee a consistently high yield, a stem, or scion, from a tree with a demonstrated capacity to produce many seeds had to be grafted onto an existing pongamia rootstock. So they studied thousands of pongamia variants, identifying and collecting the best sources of high-quality grafting stock. This not only removed the uncertainty from the yield, it also reduced the time to harvest from ten years to as little as three. In addition to scions from reliable trees, the villagers would need rootstocks for grafting, so Roshini Biotech established large nurseries to provide a steady supply.

Once the villagers had mastered the planting, grafting, and irrigation techniques, they were ready to begin. Roshini Biotech and the Himalayan Institute organized the villagers into groups and helped them qualify for low-interest loans so they could undertake the project. Roshini Biotech's research nurseries supplied the seedlings and grafting materials. The company also served as the focal point for ensuring there is enough water available to irrigate the young trees. The federal government offered subsidy grants in the form of rice so the farmers and their families would not go hungry during the start-up phase. This was instrumental in persuading the farmers to commit acreage to the pongamia project because the rice subsidy amounted to approximately three hundred kilograms per acre—more rice than can be grown on an acre of land in the region in a bad year.

As the farmers worked their fields, Reddy and his associates turned their attention to organizing and coordinating cooperative efforts. It is said that it takes a village to raise a child. It also takes a village to raise pongamia. Years of mistrust and hard times had strained the traditional bonds of fellowship that hold rural communities together. Now it was time to renew them.

Recognizing that the Himalayan Institute had made a long-term commitment to helping, the villagers joined hands to work as one to ensure their collective efforts would bear fruit. Starting with the village councils, cooperation at a grassroots level was established. Land that had once been fragmented into tiny plots and farmed by the individual owners was planted in pongamia and tended collectively. Farmers worked together to plant seedlings on land owned by the village and shared the responsibility for tending the young trees.

Another example of this newfound cooperation was the development of a community-based irrigation system. Villagers began to share the responsibility for collecting and distributing precious irrigation water. By overcoming their urge to grasp tightly to what little they had, and instead working together for the common good, the villagers took a huge step in restoring the trusting relationships that once defined their way of life.

What began in 2003 as a pilot project involving a few thousand families and ten thousand acres of pongamia trees has mushroomed. Today, more than forty thousand families are cultivating more than one hundred thousand acres of pongamia. Resilient green saplings rise from dusty red fields, transforming the landscape around hundreds of villages. Yet, the fruit of this project goes far deeper than income generation and alternative energy, for it has touched the hearts of these villagers. For them, the pongamia tree is producing seeds of hope.

Afterword
A Spiritual Vision of Life

Rolf Sovik, Psy.D.
Rolf Sovik was initiated as a pandit in the Himalayan tradition in 1987 after fifteen years of practice under the guidance of Swami Rama. Sovik also holds degrees in philosophy, history, music, Eastern Studies, and clinical psychology. He serves as the spiritual director of the Himalayan Institute in Honesdale, Pennsylvania, and is co-director with his wife, Mary Gail, of the Himalayan Institute of Buffalo, New York. He is the author of *Moving Inward: The Journey to Meditation,* the co-author of the best-selling manual *Yoga: Mastering the Basics,* and has released two CDs of relaxation practices.

THE MESSAGE OF SACRED LINK ECHOES one promoted long ago by Vedic sages. It is captured in the Vedas by the phrase *eternal order*—an order that links cultures and people of all times and places. Today, as we search for peace in a climate of strife and conflict, it is this message of common good that needs airing.

In the world of religion, each religion offers something important to its devotees, but fanaticism and isolation fostered by narrow views of religion weaken us all. In fact, the feeling that we must chase after God to find happiness is itself misleading. It promotes guilt, self-doubt, and self-condemnation, as well as the separation of spiritual life from everyday life. The great seers of humanity never believed that one culture, race, or religion was superior to another. And they emphasized again and again that it is in becoming a fully developed human being—not in negating life—that the aims of spirituality are actually realized.

The diverse authors of the Upanishads, the Jain sage Mahabir, and the Buddha all tried to awaken humans to the message that God is not in heaven but is the self-illuminating fire that shines in nature and in the heart of every being. But the habit of creating deities who live far away from daily life, of binding ourselves with rules and dogma, and of inward condemnation has proved hard to break. The tendency to run after God, and after those who claim to represent God, remains common. Insecurity and doubt persist, and even the priests and messengers of modern religions are not free from them.

The message of Sacred Link offers a bold contrast: Be strong, courageous, and broad minded. Live without fear of rules imposed by others or by convention. Stand for the highest principle of life. That principle is to live without causing harm to others or to one's own self.

Our own conscience can lead us on a path of selfless service and love for humanity. We can recognize that the light shining in every life—in plants, in animals, and in humans—is one light. Our own unique understanding of virtue will guide our conduct among the many creatures of the world. Yoga and meditation will provide us with confidence to bring this universal spiritual vision to life. In the end, the relationships that arise out of this vision will be a Sacred Link among us all.

The Himalayan Institute

The main building of the Institute headquarters near Honesdale, Pennsylvania

FOUNDED IN 1971 BY SWAMI RAMA, the Himalayan Institute has been dedicated to helping people grow physically, mentally, and spiritually by combining the best knowledge of both the East and the West.

Our international headquarters is located on a beautiful 400-acre campus in the rolling hills of the Pocono Mountains of northeastern Pennsylvania. The atmosphere here is one to foster growth, increase inner awareness, and promote calm. Our grounds provide a wonderfully peaceful and healthy setting for our seminars and extended programs. Students from all over the world join us here to attend programs in such diverse areas as hatha yoga, meditation, stress reduction, ayurveda, nutrition, Eastern philosophy, psychology, and other subjects. Whether the programs are for weekend meditation retreats, week-long seminars on spirituality, months-long residential programs, or holistic health services, the attempt here is to provide an environment of gentle inner progress. We invite you to join with us in the ongoing process of personal growth and development.

The Institute is a nonprofit organization. Your membership in the Institute helps to support its programs. Please call or write for information on becoming a member.

Programs and Services include:

- Weekend or extended seminars and workshops
- Meditation retreats and advanced meditation instruction
- Hatha yoga teachers' training
- Residential programs for self-development
- Holistic health services and pancha karma at the Institute's Center for Health and Healing
- Spiritual excursions
- Varcho Veda® herbal products
- Himalayan Institute Press
- *Yoga + Joyful Living* magazine
- Sanskrit correspondence course

A *Quarterly Guide to Programs and Other Offerings* is free within the USA. To request a copy, or for further information, call 800-822-4547 or 570-253-5551; write to the Himalayan Institute, 952 Bethany Turnpike, Honesdale, PA 18431, USA; or visit our website at www.HimalayanInstitute.org.

HIMALAYAN INSTITUTE®
PRESS

HIMALAYAN INSTITUTE PRESS has long been regarded as the resource for holistic living. We publish dozens of titles, as well as audio and videotapes that offer practical methods for living harmoniously and achieving inner balance. Our approach addresses the whole person—body, mind, and spirit—integrating the latest scientific knowledge with ancient healing and self-development techniques.

As such, we offer a wide array of titles on physical and psychological health and well-being, spiritual growth through meditation and other yogic practices, as well as translations of yogic scriptures.

Our yoga accessories include the Japa Kit for meditation practice and the Neti Pot™, the ideal tool for sinus and allergy sufferers. Our Varcho Veda® line of quality herbal extracts is now available to enhance balanced health and well-being.

Subscriptions are available to a bimonthly magazine, *Yoga + Joyful Living*, which offers thought-provoking articles on all aspects of meditation and yoga, including yoga's sister science, ayurveda.

For a free catalog, call 800-822-4547 or 570-253-5551; e-mail hibooks@HimalayanInstitute.org; fax 570-647-1552; write to the Himalayan Institute Press, 630 Main St., Suite 350, Honesdale, PA 18431-1843, USA; or visit our website at www.HimalayanInstitute.org.